Pontchartrain
BEACH

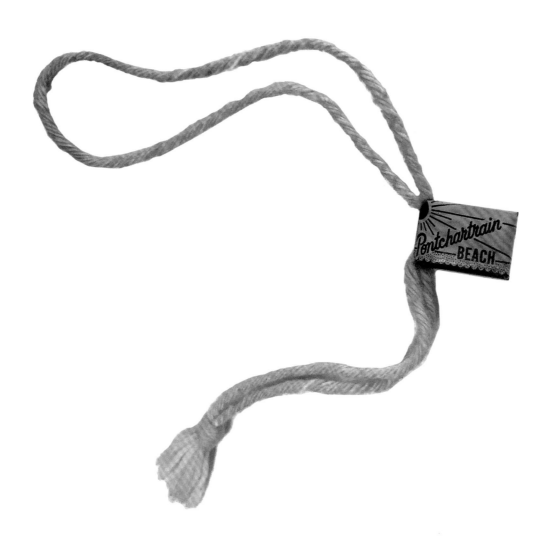

Pontchartrain BEACH

A Family Affair

Bryan Batt and Katy Danos

To hannah—
dream big + work
hard in all you do!
including having fun!
Love, Aunt Katy
11·18·2018

ENJOY THE FUN!

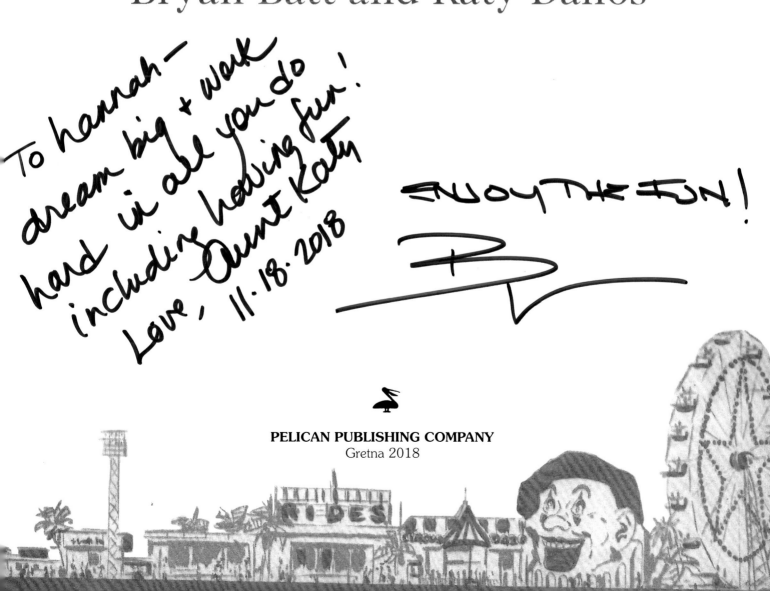

PELICAN PUBLISHING COMPANY
Gretna 2018

Library of Congress Cataloging-in-Publication Data

Names: Batt, Bryan, author. | Danos, Katy.
Title: Pontchartrain Beach : a family affair / by Bryan Batt and Katy Danos.
Description: Gretna, LA : Pelican Publishing Company, 2018. | Includes index.
Identifiers: LCCN 2017060399| ISBN 9781455621934 (hardcover : alk. paper)
  | ISBN 9781455621941 (ebook)
Subjects: LCSH: Pontchartrain Beach (New Orleans, La. : Amusement park)
| New Orleans (La.)—Social life and customs—20th century. | New Orleans
  (La.)—Biography.
Classification: LCC GV1853.3.L82 P6638 2018 | DDC 791.06/876335—dc23
LC record available at https://lccn.loc.gov/2017060399

Page 2: Art from the twenty-fifth anniversary brochure, circa 1953.

Printed in China

Published by Pelican Publishing Company, Inc.
1000 Burmaster Street, Gretna, Louisiana 70053
www.pelicanpub.com

To Leah, Hannah, Alden, Bailey, Kelly, Marie, Liza, and Henry—everything is possible with a bold imagination and an open mind

Contents

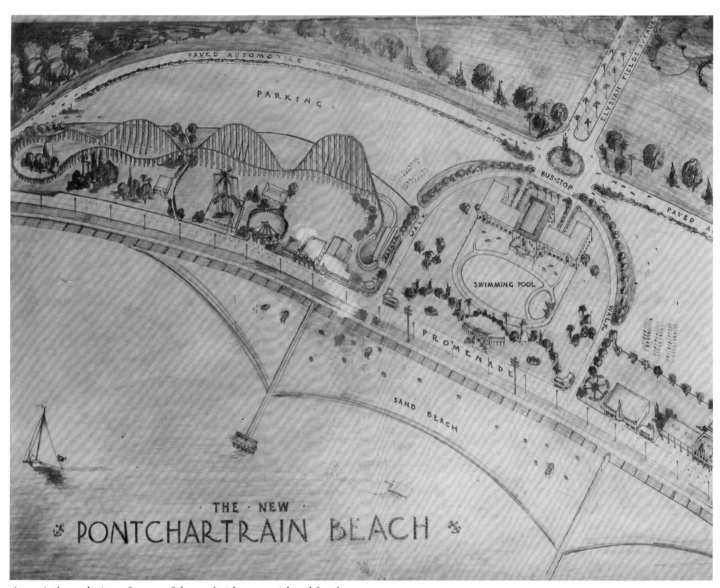

An artist's rendering of some of the early ideas considered for the new Pontchartrain Beach.

Page 6: Jay Batt commissioned a beautifully detailed realist painting by famed artist Doug Bloodworth. The unveiling at his friend Guy Lyman's New Orleans gallery was quite an event.

Introduction

At the beach, at the beach, at Pontchartrain Beach
You'll have fun, you'll have fun every day of the week.
You'll love the thrilling rides,
Laugh 'til you split your sides,
At Pontchartrain, Pontchartrain Beach.

My father's father was an iceman and he overcameth. As the story goes, my grandfather was in his horse-drawn carriage delivering ice from his family's business to the stately mansions along St. Charles Avenue when he noticed, across the neutral ground, a speeding Model T truck carrying a refrigerator. He instinctively thought, "I've got to get out of this business." Over the years, I'm sure some poetic license has been taken with the tale, but the outcome was just that; the iceman became a showman and what a showman he was. He dreamed of New Orleans having a real family amusement park, and Pontchartrain Beach was born.

I believe in magic and my grandfather, Harry J. Batt, Sr., did too. He possessed the ineffable gifts of explosive creativity and a soaring imagination. I thought he was wonderful simply because he was my grandfather, my Dad-ee, but I later realized that he was an undeniable inspiration to so many people. For me, the journey of writing this book has illuminated his indomitable and charismatic spirit again, and I have often felt his encouraging presence along the way. I am grateful for the sprinkle of his magic that lives in me, and I hope that everyone who visited Pontchartrain Beach experienced that same enchanted feeling. We all have favorite memories of our childhood, and mine will always be the exuberance and timeless joy that was the Beach. Through his example, I learned to follow my dreams with unbridled passion.

Several years ago, my brother, Jay, and I were tackling the monumental task of clearing out our late mother's home and garage. Sorting through volumes of personal letters, holiday decorations galore, and family photographs was an emotional rollercoaster. Beneath the years of sentimental rubble, we excavated several boxes simply marked *PB*. A black-and-white publicity photo of my grandfather on the Midway grabbed my heart. He was shaking my dad's and uncle's hands, signifying the passing of the Beach to the next generation. The last time I'd seen this picture, it was hanging in my father's office in the 1980s. Memorabilia erupted from the boxes. What better sign did I need to initiate this voyage?

In 2013, the Krewe of Endymion introduced the largest Mardi Gras float in history, which was an homage to Pontchartrain Beach—a masterpiece that commemorated all the wonders of the Midway. It brought tears to my eyes as I witnessed thousands upon thousands of parade-goers celebrating my grandfather's iconic gift to the city; the joy and magic were palpable. I knew then that his story had to be shared.

Initially, Katy and I toyed with the idea of a more historical approach, but we are not historians; we are storytellers. So we pulled down the safety bar, took a deep breath, and metaphorically rode the Zephyr over and over and over again. Please be our guest: ride every ride, and see every show. There are no height requirements, and "pay one price" still gets you full access to every attraction! The magical Midway is open once again on these pages. Welcome to *Pontchartrain Beach: A Family Affair!*

Bryan Batt

When something is magical, it has the power to move you in ways that may be hard to define but are indeed real. Pontchartrain Beach was magical in every way. The amusement park founded by Harry Batt, Sr., and his wife, Marguerite, in 1928 was indeed an astonishing place both literally, in all that it encompassed physically, and figuratively, in all that it means to our collective memory. A family business that has been gone since 1983 but still holds such an intensely felt place in our minds and hearts was clearly something special. With the lure of multiple draws—glistening sand, daring attractions, live entertainment, and carnival concessions—there was more than enough greatness to sustain the enterprise for over fifty years. But an inventory of the rides, attendance records, and list of celebrities who graced the Beach stage do not begin to tell the full story of this unique place and time in New Orleans history. Magic has more to do with chemistry, timing, and just the right ingredients that transform the ordinary into a universal elixir that is magnetic and enduring. Pontchartrain Beach, 1928-83, was all of this and so much more.

There seemed like no better time than our city's tricentennial to tackle the project of documenting the history of the Beach. There are so many stories to tell in New Orleans' 300-year tale, and this one, which covers so much about popular culture in twentieth-century New Orleans, beckoned us. Long before Bryan and I were born, our grandfathers knew one another. My grandfather, known as the Turtle Soup Man, delivered the dish that he was famous for at his down-the-bayou restaurant, the White Tavern, to Bryan's grandfather in the city almost weekly. For years, we have laughed about what they might be thinking as they look down on their Tulanian grandkids, and we often wonder if we are making them proud in the ways that matter most. We knew that if we didn't tell this story now, it might be lost forever.

We started our research with the grandchildren of the park's founders, knowing that they could provide a rare perspective as children living the amusement-park life as their family adventure. We rummaged through their attics and pored over trunk after trunk of newspaper clippings and souvenirs. Actual documents dating as far back as the late twenties, such as Marguerite's letters and journals and the Beach's newspaper, *Breezy Brevities,* instantly gave voice to their thoughts and motivations. It was exciting to hear from them!

Once we'd interviewed the family and had resounding support for our project, we announced through newspapers and social media that we were collecting information, photographs, and narratives that would capture the essence of the park from a myriad of ages and points of view. Of course, we studied as much as we could find about the subject, but many of the accounts were repetitive and only scratched the surface of the emotional and cultural impact that this hot-weather mecca had on our community. So we went right back to what Harry Sr. had always focused on to be successful—the people of New Orleans. These are your stories, your interviews, your scrapbooks, and your recollections. These are the right ingredients.

Harry Batt, Sr.'s compelling personality and grand achievements are best imagined with a clear understanding of what the entertainment landscape looked like during his career. Much of what might seem quaint at first glance is actually quite revolutionary in the context of its time. For one, everything about Pontchartrain Beach was new, even the ground on which it was built. In the park's heyday, there was no television in every home, much less in every room; no air conditioning, much less central air; and no shopping malls, much less the Internet. There were no technological gadgets for communicating with people without ever actually speaking to or seeing a live person or devices to provide an endless stream of visual information without ever having to leave your home or look up from your own computer. What *was* there in his time was a sweltering New Orleans seeking a respite from the heat and, later, a booming middle class and youth movement eager for social engagement and inspiration. Pontchartrain Beach presented a masterful array of communal, interactive, and participatory-driven activities that aligned perfectly with the psyche and desires of the times.

In the following pages, you will hear from former employees, performers, patrons, and friends of the Batt family and Pontchartrain Beach. We are excited to present lesser-known facts and bird's-eye views that only a family member or employee might vividly recall. We've included photographs of thrill seekers, romantics, and dreamers across the many decades in order to flood the book with the smells, sounds, and excitement of the park in a way that words can never match. Although changes in fashion, social mores, and attitudes are apparent, there is a constant that spans all of the imagery, and that is the authentic joy that is captured on film. So many family pictures were lost in Hurricane Katrina or simply have faded in humid attics over the years, but we've done our best to read the handwritten notes attached and to correctly identify people. There is very little written material about the early years, and as in most legendary tales, stories lose facts over the decades of retelling and seem to "gain" them just as fast. But by following every lead, piecing together lateral stories, and studying paperwork in the Batt family collection, we've been able to recognize Harry Batt, Sr.'s singular contribution to a magical city we love so dearly.

We hope that in reading our book, you enjoy a nostalgic look back, gather new understandings about the Beach in its day, and are inspired to think about the future of family entertainment and communication with a pioneering mindset. We know that is what Harry would be doing.

Katy Danos

Chapter 1
In the Good Old Summertime

In 1903, when Harry Batt entered the world, New Orleans was the most vibrant and prosperous city in the South. As a wealthy American port city in an abundant agricultural region, New Orleans had strong financial ties to Boston, Chicago, and New York, as well as to the rest of the world. The French Quarter brimmed with fine restaurants, theatre, and commerce that reflected our multicultural artistic intellect and soul, and the docks and warehouses along the Mississippi River and the French Market bustled with activity. Well-heeled urban dwellers from Uptown and the Garden District flocked to nearby Lake Pontchartrain in the summer to escape the city's oppressive heat and risk of disease. At the turn of the twentieth century, New Orleans was exploding with growth and joie de vivre.

The Batt family immigrated from Germany to the big easy land of opportunity in the mid-1800s, and Harry's grandfather, hardworking and enterprising, built the city's very first ice manufacturing plant in 1883. In this sweltering town before air conditioning, he recognized a market. New Orleans was in dire need of one very hot commodity—ice. He founded the Home Ice Company and the business thrived, making and delivering ice to Newcomb College and Tulane University, the mansions that lined St. Charles Avenue, and the resort settlements that dotted the southern shore of Lake Pontchartrain. When Harry was born, his father, John, was at the helm of the company, and the Batt family was deeply entrenched in a solid middle-class lifestyle. Just like the blossoming city, Harry's future was bright.

By 1916, World War I was well under way, and although the demand for ice remained healthy, the supply of employable men did not. The influenza and yellow-fever epidemics of prior decades, coupled with a world at war, meant that there was simply not enough manpower. The men were all enlisted. So at the age of thirteen, Harry left school to work alongside his father in the family business. This marked the end of his formal education and the beginning of a lifetime of learning.

Opposite: Harry Batt, Sr., and a colleague admiring the Space Wheel, a rare double Ferris wheel installed in 1958 at the Beach. It is the only one of its kind ever built and it thrilled riders through the early 1960s. It is now being restored by Drew Expositions.

A rare photograph of a couple posed with the historic Smoky Mary at the turn of the twentieth century.

Young Harry came of age in a postwar New Orleans filled with hope. He delivered blocks of ice to a booming French Quarter arts scene, rivaled only by New York's Greenwich Village, and to a flourishing Canal Street, one of the widest commercial thoroughfares in the world. The Mississippi River teemed with steamboats alive with music and dancing. He also provided ice for the burgeoning resort settlements along the lake, such as Old Spanish Fort at the mouth of Bayou St. John and Milneburg at the end of Elysian Fields. Spanish Fort, the city's most upscale recreation area, boasted a hotel, restaurants, dance pavilions, and a casino. Prominent families spent weeks at their summer houses enjoying cool lake breezes, boating, and bathing. A small Coney Island-style amusement park with a rollercoaster, concessions, and a penny arcade provided family entertainment. Farther east, Milneburg, the older of the two, was the jazz hotspot, where the speakeasy set from all walks of life gathered nightly for drinking and dancing the Charleston. Although the temperature at both resorts was exactly the same, the vibe at the latter was far cooler.

Harry married Marguerite Spraul, of German descent, in 1924, and like most young couples of the era, they recognized the winds of exhilarating change in the air. The Roaring Twenties were marked by astounding technological innovation and social progress. Inventions such as the radio brought world news and music into homes for the first time, which banded citizens together. Mass production of the Model T Ford made automobiles more attainable, and the inconceivable idea of air travel would soon take flight. In 1927, the country saw the first talkie—*The Jazz Singer*—a motion picture that ended the silent movie era and revolutionized the industry. A developing Hollywood captured everyone's imagination.

A shoreline view of Spanish Fort Amusement Park.

Harry was buoyed by this invigorating sense of freedom and creativity, but when General Electric announced in the mid-1920s their new home automated refrigerator with ice-cube compartments, he could see the writing on the wall. Married with children on the way and a personality wired for change, he knew that the family business had to diversify. He convinced his father to sublease a few concessions and the arcade at Spanish Fort and to invest in three rides there—the Caterpillar, the Bug, and the Flying Scooter. And just like that, the Batts were in the business of show.

It wasn't long before the other primary amusement operators, laden with debt, realized that they did not have the capital to continuously update the park. When business at Spanish Fort faltered, the other operators simply walked away. By default, Harry, in order to protect the Batts' initial investment, took over the remaining rides, including the popular Wildcat and the Whip. It was a risky move and his father thought he was crazy, but he entertained no other outcome except for success.

The rickety old park was built on pilings and stilts on boggy ground in the shallows of the lake. A long boardwalk extended far out into the waters to the bathing area, which included an antiquated wooden bathhouse. Everything was outdated, and Harry was restless. Intent on bringing the newest and the best to his enterprise, he booked the showiest circus acts of the day, updated the arcade games, and expanded the concessions. He spared no expense. When the park opened for the 1928 season, it had a brand-new name—Pontchartrain Beach—and a stunning, modern, grand entrance presenting an ambitious identity.

Two peas in a pod. Marguerite and Harry Batt, Sr., in the Roaring Twenties, sporting matching swim attire on the Spanish Fort boardwalk.

A very early airplane ride at the Spanish Fort Amusement Park, circa 1920s.

The original entrance of Pontchartrain Beach, circa 1928.

Harry had long been intrigued by family stories of the 1884 World's Cotton Centennial Exposition, which was held at what is present-day Audubon Park in New Orleans. So when the Chicago World's Fair, known as "A Century of Progress," opened in 1933, he immediately jumped on a train to experience this opportunity of a lifetime. The fair celebrated technology and its infinite possibilities, Art Deco architecture, modern dream cars, and innovative products for the home. And the streamlined bullet-shaped train called the Zephyr, which was presented with the greatest of fanfare, ignited his creative DNA and fueled his dynamic energy. The Zephyr was lightning fast, a stunning work of art and design symbolizing great prosperity and American ingenuity. With great zeal, he set about studying every detail of the fair. This pinnacle experience was etched in his powerful brain. In looking at his astonishing career, it is not overreaching to say that the World's Fair of 1933 was a defining moment in his life; it informed his worldview and established a blueprint for his future. The exhibition's motto—"Science Finds, Industry Applies, Man Adapts"—became his creed, and he returned to New Orleans emboldened with advanced ideas for Pontchartrain Beach.

A poster from the Chicago World's Fair.

Below: The Wildcat wooden rollercoaster circa 1920s-30s.

Following spread: A Pontchartrain Beach postcard from the 1930s. Bathers enjoy the lake and families stroll on the boardwalk.

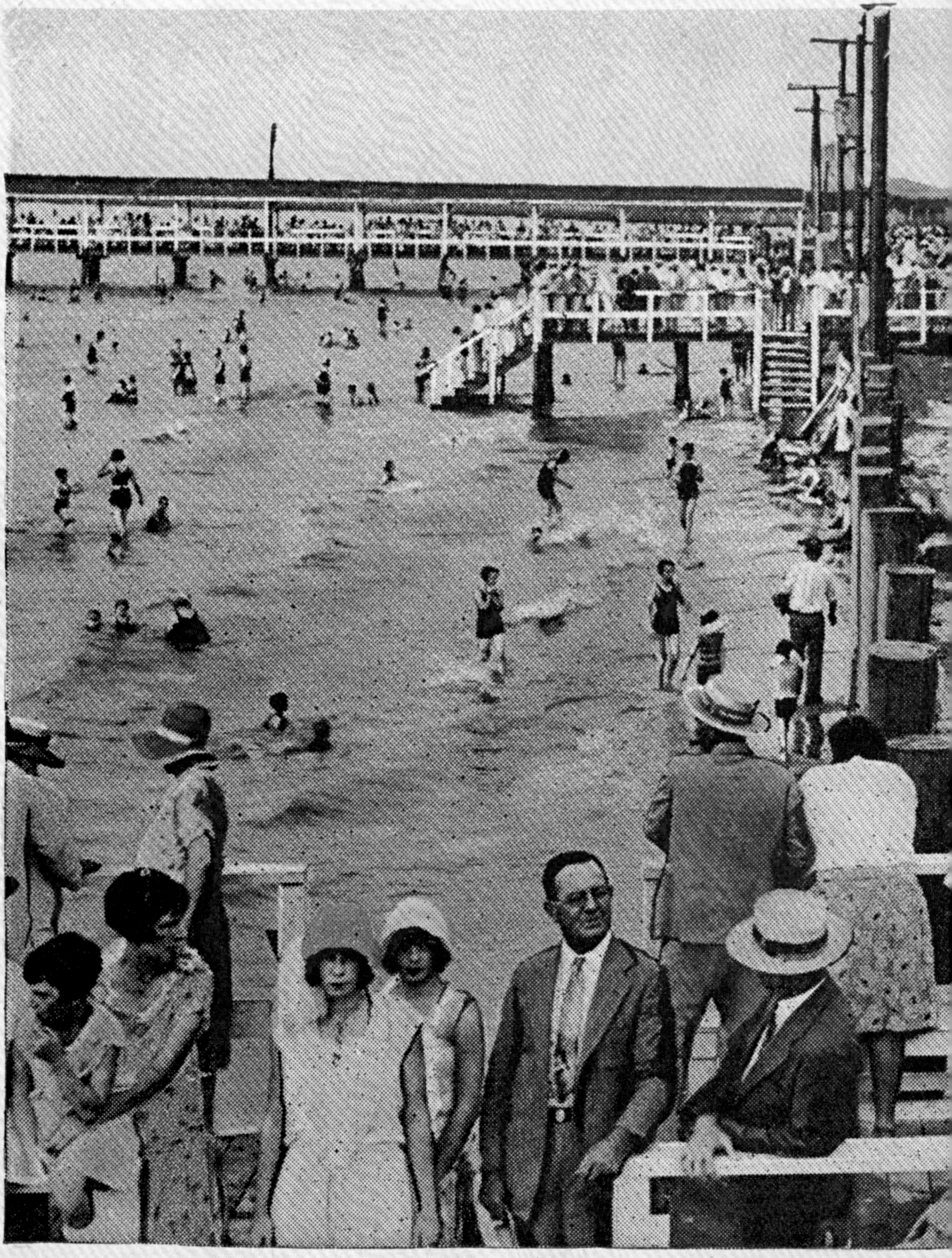

30652

The prewar boardwalk in all its glory, 1935.

WPA workers in front of the Milneburg Lighthouse. In this exact spot, Harry Batt, Sr., built the amusement park of his dreams.

The depression was a brutal time for any business, but the World's Fair was full of hope and so was Harry. Because the New Deal pumped millions of dollars and hundreds of jobs into New Orleans, the city was buffered from some of the harshest realities. Marguerite worked diligently alongside her husband, handling all of the accounting. They commuted from Nashville Avenue Uptown to Pontchartrain Beach at Spanish Fort daily. It was ten miles each way and the roads were by no means state of the art, but the extensive federal projects under way all around them were. With their keen eye, this did not go unnoticed. The Orleans Levee Board, with funding from the Works Progress Administration, was undertaking a massive reclamation of lakefront land, and ambitious construction projects put hundreds of men to work. The Elysian Fields corridor was being developed into a four-lane scenic roadway connecting the heart of the city to Milneburg for the very first time, which transformed the area's accessibility.

In such a difficult time in our world's history, magnificent progress in the New Orleans lakefront landscape was made, including bridges, a new seawall, and developed recreational acreage. Enlightened by the spectacular Chicago World's Fair, which was also built on filled-in lakeshore land, Harry understood exactly what was happening and envisioned what was sure to come—an explosion of growth for neighborhoods we now know as Gentilly and Lakeview. This was the land of the future and the blank canvas that Harry needed to fully realize his vision. Like the Zephyr train that Harry so admired at the fair, he was determined that Pontchartrain Beach rocket forward. In competition with other prominent businessmen, he pitched his plan to the Levee Board, detailing what he would provide the community if he was awarded the twenty-year lease on the newly available fifty-four acres of lakefront land. The city planners were committed to maintaining Milneburg as a recreational area; therefore, his aspirational plan of dredging the lake and trucking white sand from the Gulf shore to create a sparkling beachfront was appealing. But his unbridled zeal and promise to build a world-class amusement park unparalleled in the South, if not the country, is what won them over. The Levee Board was wild about Harry, and a fifty-year partnership commenced that exceeded all expectations.

A bird's-eye view of construction at the Beach's new location at the end of Elysian Fields Avenue, circa 1938.

LAKE FRONT
NEWS

The Times-Picayune
NEW ORLEANS STATES

PONTCHARTRAIN BEACH
OPENING

SECTION SIX   NEW ORLEANS, SUNDAY, JUNE 18, 1939   SECTION SIX

NEW PONTCHARTRAIN BEACH OPENS TODAY

Harry opened his "new" Pontchartrain Beach at the end of Elysian Fields in the spring of 1939. The park had a Deco-inspired Midway complete with a penny arcade, concessions, and eight rides, some which he brought over from the old location such as the Sea Planes and the Whip. But the piece de resistance was the appropriately named, iconic Zephyr, a show-stopping, state-of-the-art, wooden rollercoaster that is still considered today to be one of the finest and most thrilling rides ever built. Although the Second World War was looming, Harry approached his commitment to the citizens of New Orleans with boundless enthusiasm, relentless confidence, and a laser-sharp vision for his amusement park that would not be deterred. Harry had always been fearless about making the most of any and all opportunities, and he made the challenging times work for him. Wartime facilities such as the Naval Air Station and forty-eight-hour-leave tent cities erected on these new lakefront grounds, along with nearby Camp Leroy Johnson and Camp Polk, ensured a steady flow of patrons. Men in uniform received half-price tickets on all games and rides. Harry also allowed the military to use his parking lot and beach for drills, and he created endless wartime-related drives, contests, activities, and incentives that not only kept the park afloat but also boosted local morale.

World War II servicemen enjoying the Midway and the Cockeyed Circus attraction, 1942.

Harry Batt, Sr., circa 1950s, "talking rides" with colleagues—
one of his favorite things to do anytime, anyplace.

The undisputable Pontchartrain Beach heyday was from 1944 to 1979. The rollercoaster of a ride was marked by eras of sweeping positive change not only in New Orleans but the world at large, such as the baby boom and desegregation. There were also times of great challenge for a family-owned amusement park, such as the increasing lake pollution and the rise of the litigation and liability mentality. The Beach experienced it all, keeping its gates open until 1983. Harry and Marguerite Batt, and later their two sons, Harry Jr. and John, delivered an unquantifiable measure of joy, romance, and entertainment to the city of New Orleans for over fifty-five years. As New Orleans, a town truly like no other, celebrates her 300th birthday, we celebrate Harry, a New Orleanian with unparalleled imagination and contributions to this astounding American city.

How fitting that the most popular song in the country in 1903, the year that Harry was born, was "In the Good Old Summertime." It was destiny.

There was a train called Smoky Mary . . .

The glamor and history of old New Orleans has been portrayed in endless pageant and story, but never more graphically than in its jazz music and song.

Significant it is that the famous "Basin St. Blues" became "Milneburg Joys" when the romantic folk of old New Orleans left their cares behind as they boarded the ancient train, Smoky Mary, for the present site of Pontchartrain Beach.

Today the old Milneburg lighthouse stands in Kiddieland at the center of Pontchartrain Beach as a beacon and a reminder of the joys of old Milneburg. The jazz bands that blared their siren song over the waters from the Milneburg camps have since been tempered. The iron rails that led Smoky Mary and her joyous cargo to Milneburg have now been transformed into majestic paved highways, with modern overpasses and underpasses. Smoky Mary herself has long ago given way to modern buses and the horseless carriage which she once looked upon with much disdain.

And the Milneburg joys have been multiplied many fold at Pontchartrain Beach around the hallowed lighthouse that treasures memories of a glamorous and fun-loving past.

The Men Behind Pontchartrain Beach

JOHN W. BATT

HARRY J. BATT

HARRY J. BATT, JR.

Three generations of the Batt family have been active in the management of Pontchartrain Beach.

John W. Batt, a lifelong resident and businessman of uptown New Orleans, brought a keen interest in children and recreation facilities into the development of Pontchartrain Beach. Since his death in 1940, his memory is honored with an annual outing for the orphaned and underprivileged children of his native city at the Beach.

Harry J. Batt, Sr. became president of Playland Amusements, Inc. following the passing of his father. His energy and spirit has been the dominant factor in making Pontchartrain Beach a civic asset and the South's finest recreational beach resort. He has served as president of the National Association of Parks, Pools and Beaches during 1949 and 1950, and was awarded the Andrew McSwigan trophy for the most outstanding service to the industry in 1949. He is at present chairman of the Special Tax committee of the NAPPB.

Harry Batt's two sons, Harry Batt, Jr. as secretary-treasurer and assistant manager, and John A. Batt, as vice-president, are now carrying on the managerial principles of their grandfather and father before them.

JOHN A. BATT

Pontchartrain Beach's twenty-fifth anniversary brochure paid tribute to all of the Beach's men as well as the Smoky Mary and Milneburg Lighthouse.

A thrill is a tingling and exquisite sensation and I'm happy to say that the business of supplying thrills to folks is the most satisfying thrill I know. I haven't ever lost any zest for it. No youngster ever quite forgets their first thrill on a merry-go-round and no teenager the thrill of a rollercoaster.

Harry Batt, Sr.

You don't know what you've got until it's gone. Pontchartrain Beach had a soul.
Holly Ghere

Bathers and lifeguards, early 1930s.

An aerial view reflecting the boomtime development of the park and outlying areas circa 1940s.

Bobby-soxers flirting with sailors as they wait in line for the photo booth.

The most popular spot on the Midway for children's snapshots was the iconic clown head, circa 1950s.

PONTCHARTRAIN BEACH

A 1950s aerial view of the park and expanding neighborhoods in Gentilly.

It felt modern and magical. It was like no
place else in New Orleans.

Arthur Wehl

Pamphlet art celebrating the twenty-fifth
anniversary.

Chapter 2
Dancing Through Life

There are five times in your life when you come to Pontchartrain Beach. First with your parents, then you're here with your friends as a youth; you come when you're courting, then you bring your own kids; and finally, you're back at the Beach with your grandchildren.

Harry Batt, Jr., 1979

This is pretty much how it went for the Batt family. Introduced by their mothers, Harry married Marguerite when he was twenty-one and she was eighteen. "Mothers know best" certainly applies here, because these kindred spirits were happily married for over fifty years. With two dynamic and inquisitive personalities and more in common than many couples, they were equally drawn to adventure and change. In the beginning, Marguerite was the Pontchartrain Beach cashier and a meticulous bookkeeper. From a family of seven sisters of modest means, she was no stranger to frugality, and she was a visionary in her own right. When the time came for the Batts to make the ambitious move from Old Spanish Fort to Elysian Fields, Harry was rightfully concerned about having enough capital. But Marguerite had squirreled away funds that even Harry didn't know about, making the transition far smoother than either expected. No finer match for Harry is imaginable.

The amusement park they built was competitive on an international scale; there was nothing regional or even national about their way of thinking. Harry learned everything about the business by visiting every zoo, fair, and carnival he could in the States—the 1936 Texas Centennial Fair, 1937 Great Lakes Exposition, and 1939 New York World's Fair—returning with novel ideas to take the Beach to new heights. With annual international trips to the Munich Oktoberfest, the Canadian Exposition, and storied parks such as Tivoli Gardens in Denmark, he soon became a leading expert in the industry. Both Harry and Marguerite possessed pioneering instincts and were energized by modernity, but Harry's quest for knowledge and inspiration was unrivaled. They both set the highest bar for their endeavors and pursued their dreams with unabashed enthusiasm. Every season had to be newer, bigger, better than the last, and with her birthday on New Year's Eve, Marguerite greeted each new year with that confident attitude. "Complacency" was not part of their vocabulary.

Opposite: Marguerite and Harry Batt, Sr., entertaining at home. Dancing was a lifelong shared passion.

The Batts enjoying retirement as they traveled around the world in the mid-sixties.

Dependent on the weather, a short twenty-week season, and the mood of the country, the summer amusement-park business was intense and tricky. The Beach, confined to the available acreage leased from the city, was unlikely to ever expand in size; therefore, Harry focused on layering in value after value in every popular form of family entertainment. And neither he nor Marguerite ever lost touch with the mindset of working-class families. As Harry often said, a ride investment was hundreds of thousands of dollars, but the return relied on nickels and dimes.

Their two sons, Harry Jr. and John, worked in all phases of the park their entire lives except while they were in college or active air-force duty. Harry Sr. was proud to be able to give so many young people their first jobs, and that included his own sons. The work was hard and sweltering, including stints in the snowball shed, ticket counter, and maintenance shops. As the boys matured, they learned the advertising, promotions, and financial aspects of the family business, and in time they were named president and vice president of Playland Amusements, the company's official name. The brothers were accustomed to the grueling schedule set by their father—at work by 7:00 A.M. and home at 11:00 P.M. during the high season—but their new wives, Fay and Gayle, were not. John actually did not get home until 1:00 A.M. because he had the late shift, which included closing the Bali Ha'i restaurant and tucking the park in for the night. It was several summers into marriage before the women, with five rambunctious children between them, successfully lobbied Harry Sr. for one day off a week for their husbands to spend time with their families. Dynamic personalities run in the family.

All of the Batt grandchildren, Harry III, David, Barbara, Jay, and Bryan, have poignant memories, humorous stories, and insightful reflections about growing up with this illustrious amusement park as their playground. Seen through their lens and unique perspectives, we are offered a rare peek into a one-of-a-kind family business that spanned almost six decades. Pontchartrain Beach was indeed like a second home to New Orleanians, but for this close-knit group it was strictly a family affair.

David Batt, Harry Batt, Jr., Fay Vilac Batt, Barbara Batt, Harry Batt III, John Batt, Jr. (Jay), Gayle Mackenroth Batt, Bryan Batt, John Batt, early 1960s at Fay and Harry's home.

On the drive home from an Eastern Seaboard trip, Dad-ee decided we should stop off at the Newport Jazz Fest to say hi to Louis Armstrong. I couldn't believe he actually knew this jazz legend—unbelievable!

Harry Batt III

Gathered at Fay and Harry's home, 1960s.

The five grandchildren at Harry and Marguerite's fiftieth wedding anniversary celebration at the New Orleans Country Club, 1974.

Mom-ee [Marguerite] was the best. She was warm, fun loving, and family oriented. To the outside world, it was all Dad-ee; but in our world, she was the backbone. She was strong willed and could totally keep up with him, and she was no stranger to hard work. She kept the books in the early years and maintained all the written correspondence. They were 100 percent in it together. Mom-ee had an enormous heart and was dedicated to family. All of her sisters had jobs if they wanted one. She was traditional in many senses, leaving many things "to the men," but she was a force and totally on the ball. My parents traveled the world together. I've often said that if I could live my life as she lived hers, it would be such an honor.

Barbara Batt Claiborne

My grandfather was an amazing man, and I admired him greatly. He cut a huge swath and was a bit flamboyant, almost flashy; however, he was completely grounded. He could talk to anyone about anything and loved to learn by truly listening during conversations with people from all walks of life. He did not believe that anyone was beneath him. Although he was an extremely well read and highly self-educated man, I think he may have felt slightly inferior about not having a formal degree. Perhaps that's why he was always so supportive of Delgado Community College.

Jay Batt

Well Dressed

Both my mother and grandmother were very sentimental. They loved to celebrate family traditions and create new ones. While expecting her long-awaited first child, rather than buy a christening dress, Mom asked Mom-ee if she would make one. The result was exquisite and priceless; the hand embroidery and miniscule tucks are nothing short of masterful. She even painstakingly embroidered my brother's and later my name and christening dates on the slip, in my mother's signature script. Since Mom considered it a work of art and love, she proudly displayed it, framed in a shadowbox. When the time came, she was overjoyed for her granddaughters to continue the tradition.

Bryan Batt

Harry Batt, Sr., holding Jay at his christening reception, 1961.

Marguerite cuddling Bryan and Jay, early sixties.

Beanbags to Broadway

*I*n the seventies, my somewhat-retired grandparents moved one midcentury-modern house away from ours on a cozy tree-lined cul-de-sac in Lake Vista. Harry Sr. was only retired in the sense that he did not inhabit his swanky art-deco office at the Beach on a daily basis, but he and Marguerite continued to be a major force in all of our lives. Encouragement should have been their middle names; they were always inquisitive as to what we were learning in our activities, both academic and extracurricular. In sixth grade, my class had an economics fair. Groups of students created, produced, and advertised products to sell at the fair, all to learn the basics of a free-market economy. My group decided to design festive beanbags made from scraps of fabric. I volunteered Mom-ee's sewing expertise, but she wisely declined, knowing that labor is expensive and part of the equation. Instead, she taught me how to sew the beanbags myself, and she threw in rental of her Singer machine as gratis. There was no mention of gender issues regarding a boy sewing. Maybe they knew something I didn't know just yet, but this was viewed strictly as business.

At around this time, my love of the theatre blossomed and I was cast in several shows at NORD Theatre. I learned much later that Dad-ee was one of the founders of the New Orleans Recreation Department program. He nicknamed me Little Hambone, and he and Mom-ee saw me in almost every local performance. After he passed away, Mom-ee continued to support my love of theatre arts. Once again, she seemed to know more about me than I did—or was willing to admit at the time. Towards the end of her life, at the close of my senior year at Tulane, she told one of her night sitters, "Well, I think my grandson Bryan may be 'that way' . . . and if John Batt doesn't help him move to New York and become an actor, I will!" Sadly, she died right after my graduation, and I lost my father four months later. Neither got to see me on Broadway in my first show, *Starlight Express*. Every night while in the wings of the Gershwin Theatre, anxiously anticipating my entrance on roller skates, I sent a little prayer up to them, and I knew they were there.

Bryan

Dancing Through Life

Bryan's second birthday party, 1965. Left to right: Marguerite, Harry Sr., Bryan, and Hazel Mackenroth, his maternal grandmother.

My wife is my greatest asset. I've enjoyed her confidence, trust, and good counsel for almost fifty years.

Harry Batt, Sr., speaking at a 1970 convention

I don't know why you hire a promotions man. You have all the ideas.

Marguerite Batt

Hazel, John, and Marguerite at Bali Ha'i at the Beach's closing-night party, 1983.

Before the Parade Passes By

I inherited my flair for the theatrical from both sides of my family, but the gene for "putting on a show" definitely came from my grandfather. At an early age, I would stage puppet shows in my bedroom. All kids do this, but mine developed into dazzling floorshows prominently featured at my parents' cocktail parties. My early works matured into original plays staged in our backyard, starring any neighborhood friends who would actually commit to my rehearsal schedule. Along the way, I would convince my dad to provide the raw materials necessary for the sets, but he would often take it a step further. As if by magic, my drawings would be realized by the Beach artists, and the makeshift backyard amphitheater on Rail Street was in a league of its own.

My annual Fourth of July parade was my crowning glory. As an eight-year-old, I asked Santa for several floats of my own design for the newly formed "krewe" that would parade on or near Independence Day. And as always, Santa came through. I never once questioned how all this patriotic fabulousness made it down the chimney. The krewe was made up of family, school friends, neighborhood pals, and Little League teammates. Basically, if you had a costume, a uniform, or anything red, white, and blue, you were in. Under the broiling July sun, my parade would roll throughout the three short streets of Lake Vista and its cul-de-sacs. The event was covered by both the *New Orleans Times-Picayune* and the *States Item,* as well as several local news stations. Who knew that the North Pole's PR connections reached all the way to the Deep South? My love of theatrical pageantry was sealed and there was no turning back. After three years of the spectacular Krewe of Patriots, the organization disbanded when I was cast in *Li'l Abner* at NORD Theatre and had to make a decision . . . the U.S.A. or Dogpatch!

Bryan

Krewe of Patriots: Louisiana lieutenant governor presenting "Uncle Sam" with an honorary state senator's certificate, at Bryan's Fourth of July parade, 1973.

Top center: Bryan as Uncle Sam and Mary Beth Romig as Lady Liberty, 1973.

Bryan and Jay building a float in the Beach's storeroom, 1972.

Left to right: Campbell McCool, Seamus Thouhey, and Jimmy Brown, signing the Declaration of Independence, 1973.

Officially handing the family business down to the next generation, mid-1960s.

The O.G.

Some of the tales about traveling with my grandparents are legendary in our family. The story that we all loved to hear over and over again was how Dad-ee got the nickname "O.G." He was the original O.G., a nickname he loathed.

In 1963, the Harry Batt, Srs., treated my parents and Aunt Fay and Uncle Harry to a glamorous European tour complete with steamer trunks, hatboxes, and bellhops. It was to be first class all the way, but it was made clear there would be no rest for the weary. Harry Sr. took pride in the fact that the "young set" would find it hard to keep up with him, both mentally and physically. He exercised, took long walks, and ate healthily long before it was the trend. In short, he did everything to stay young and, to put it mildly, Harry J. Batt, Sr., was not going to go gentle into that good night. True to form, Dad-ee doubled down on his reading and research about all things European in order to make this pilgrimage unforgettable.

In London, he hired a noted historian and tour guide who came highly recommended. As the guide explained various points of interest in great detail, Dad-ee, as was his nature, interjected his vast knowledge on almost every subject. The guide displayed the utmost British gentility as he kindly endured the many interruptions and grand pontifications. This went on for several days, with the guide summoning more patience and fortitude than a Buckingham Palace guard. Finally, under the sacred vaults of Westminster Abbey, he cracked. "If the Old Gentleman would allow me to finish my statement, then ask questions, it would be most appreciated." Thus the audacious nickname of O.G. was born. Harry Batt, Sr., was never at a loss for words, but being called "Old" left him speechless and hit way below his shiny patent-leather belt.

Bryan

Hotel, Motel, Holiday Inn

For years, my Batt cousins kept my brother and me spellbound with their stories of their travels with Dad-ee. Finally, in the summer of 1975, our day had come. It was as if we'd won the *Price Is Right* showcase—an all-expenses-paid grand tour of the Great Amusement Parks of the Midwest and Eastern Seaboard. A busman's holiday if ever there was one. The plan was to fly to Chicago, rent a car, and hit the road and wide-open spaces—just us guys. In those days, a family entourage accompanied you to the departure gate. So there we were—two adolescent boys in conservative navy blazers and the most dapper septuagenarian ever to board a Braniff Airlines flight. In true Dad-ee fashion, he sported spectator wingtip oxfords, a hounds-tooth fedora, and a flashy Countess Mara tie. As we said our farewells, my dad slipped me some extra cash, a boys' version of mad money, and Mom and Mom-ee blew kisses that masked any trepidation they had for our mortal souls.

Dad-ee was a whirlwind force of nature, possessing three times our combined energy and stamina. It took us a few days to get with his program. We were early to rise and out the door driving from state to state, park to park, rollercoaster to rollercoaster, hotel to motel for nearly a month! Jay and I were on our best behavior. Rising to the occasion, we acted like gentlemen, and any sibling rivalry dissipated. We each valued Dad-ee's approval and reveled in the attention he bestowed on us. He had the unique gift of making each of us feel special.

During the long drives, Jay and O.G. would discuss politics, women, and current events, while our topics were centered around the aesthetics of amusement parks. He enjoyed our "rap sessions" as much as we did. Nothing compares to having a real conversation with a grandfather you so admire.

We hit Marriott's Great America, Busch Gardens, Kings Dominion, Cedar Point, and more. Welcome to Illinois, Ohio, New Jersey, and Pennsylvania. At each park, Dad-ee was greeted and treated like a rock star. We knew he was a big deal to us, but it was eye opening to see how respected he was all over the country. And he was impressive. He walked with such purpose and imposing huge strides that it left me scrambling and humming the seventies pop song "Daddy Don't You Walk So Fast." And he lived up to his reputation of being a speed demon and horrible driver. Late one fateful night while barreling down the highway, he missed several exits near downtown Philadelphia. Instead of circling back, he actually drove the car in reverse in the shoulder lane for what seemed like an eternity. After several failed attempts to get back on track, he finally admitted we were lost. Dad-ee decided to stop and ask for directions from some dudes who looked like extras cut from a *Kojak* episode. He exited the car, asked for directions, and we were off. In shock, we questioned his judgment, to which he plainly stated, "Boys, if you know how to talk to people, you can talk to anyone."

At Great Adventure Amusement Park in New Jersey, we saw something truly great. O.G. couldn't wait to take us on the Safari Journey, since Africa was one of his favorite places to travel. And, boy, did we learn about the call of the wild. Ten yards from our cart, two lusty rhinos attempted to mate. Dad-ee was grabbing for the camera, Jay was on the floor in hysterics, and I was mesmerized. Marlin Perkins never covered anything like this on Mutual of Omaha's *Wild Kingdom*.

My favorite memory of that wonderful trip was at the last motel. While the O.G. was at a meeting, Jay and I swam and hung around the pool. The foxy teenaged lifeguard was a brick house and a potential fourth Charlie's Angel. Later, Jay casually brought this crush to Dad-ee's attention. At dinner that night, we noticed an extra place setting. Imagine our surprise when we were introduced to the goddess of the pool. Fox on the run; Dad-ee got it done!

Bryan

I'm Gonna Wait 'Til the Midnight Hour

I was quite mischievous in high school and college. In 1981, I was on a double date and after quite a few drinks, we decided to drive out to the Beach in the wee hours of the night. Everything was closed, so I tipped the watchman to allow us in. I knew how the place worked. The first stop was the photo booth, then the bumper cars, and we even rode the Zephyr. What the hell was I thinking? I thought I'd gotten away with the caper, but the guard eventually spilled the beans. Dad hit the roof! I had never seen him so furious and he read me the riot act. As punishment, I had to report to the main offices to apologize to my uncle Harry and the guard face to face, and I was grounded for the remainder of the summer. My new assignment was in the sanitation department as a "volunteer." Every morning from six o'clock until opening, I cleaned the food stations, bathrooms, and dumpsters in the dog days of summer. My nostrils were never the same. Lesson learned.

Jay

The main offices were housed on the lower floor of this art-deco building at the Beach. A separate entrance was used for Marguerite and Harry's private soundproofed living quarters on the second floor. A glamorous Lucite and cypress spiraling staircase led guests to their uber-chic apartment, decorated in all things modern, fashionable, and South Sea inspired.

The Beach was a great lure to get friends to come out "all the way to the lakefront." We had open passes and could ride the rides as often as we desired. Although some friends would encourage us to use our position to cut the lines, we very rarely did. Dad considered it rude and never wanted to offend the patrons. It was a great way to grow up. Sort of like a huge playground on steroids right in our backyard.

Jay

Harry Batt, Jr., and John Batt on the Skyride for a 1970s publicity shoot.

As children, we rode our bikes on the Midway all winter while no one was there. No other kids lived there, so we played with the children of traveling circus performers. Dad worked from ten in the morning until one in the morning during the intense four-month season, but he came home every night for dinner. We never took family vacations during the summer; we did that at Christmas. I thought the whole world was like this.

Harry III

I worked several summers in guest relations answering phones. When the weather was bad, we would hide, because Dad was as cranky as a bear. I'd have to answer in a perky singsong voice, "No, it's not raining out here!" so that customers would still come that day.

Barbara

Pontchartrain Beach was my "true friend" litmus test. If kids were just as happy to climb trees in my backyard, they were in.

Bryan

The Tale of the Traveling Jacket

Harry Batt, Sr., loved fashion. He wasn't the man in the gray flannel suit nor the man in white linen; he was his own haberdashery dream come true. More Rat Pack than Repp Tie, he had suits custom made in Hong Kong and never met a pair of spectators or dazzling cufflinks he didn't like. He stood out in any crowd, and he liked it that way. I will admit that often he was a tad flashy; but every now and then, he would sport a getup that would have made Old Blue Eyes green. For his fortieth wedding anniversary, Dad-ee's tailor made him a silk shantung dinner jacket, cabernet red with black velvet lapels; this bespoke was smokin'. Many years later, when he passed away, each grandchild was given some of his sentimental things, and all I could think of was that red jacket. It began its second life on my sixteen-year-old shoulders at a midnight screening of *The Rocky Horror Picture Show* and on Jay when he wore it to Sub Debs in his senior year in high school. The jacket continued to stop the show when I sang "Mack the Knife" at the Tulanians Fall Concert. Many years later, my husband, Tom Cianfichi, wore it to my opening night of *Sunset Boulevard* on Broadway, which was the night Jay proposed to my sister-in-law, Andree. Whatever Dad-ee spent on that jacket, the return on his initial investment was priceless.

Bryan

Bryan's opening night of Broadway's Sunset Boulevard. *Left to right: Jay, Andree Wood, Tom, Bryan, and Gayle, 1994.*

Top: Harry and Marguerite joined by Gayle and John for their fortieth wedding anniversary, 1964.

The Last Ride

As a kid, I found it difficult to understand why from Easter Sunday until Labor Day, I rarely saw my own father. His job was all consuming. In the off-season, his interests—sports and typical guy stuff—aligned effortlessly with my older brother's passions. Being that I was artistic and theatrical by nature, our only common thread could have ended with our mutual love of Mel Brooks movies. However, there were two words that permanently cemented me to my father—Pontchartrain Beach. Through the park, he found a way to nurture my imagination and creativity.

For Halloween, I would create a haunted house in our garage, and Dad made sure it was spectacular. I worked up a floorplan and he would go the extra mile to ensure that I had the most gruesome of props. For the Batt family, all holiday decorations were of utmost importance, but Christmas was the apex. One particular year, Dad commissioned the German artist who was in residency at the Beach to create our very own Santa's Workshop. Life-sized wooden cutouts of elves and reindeer, painted in a dazzling and detailed Old World style, pranced across our front lawn. To this day, I still close my eyes and dream about this magical winter wonderland.

I fondly remember lying on the shag carpet in our den, sketching ideas for new rides and attractions while watching *The Carol Burnett Show* with my family. I thought one of my designs was exceptionally cool, so I got right to work constructing a Lego mockup of my very own thrill ride. When I showed it to my dad, he was unusually receptive and genuinely impressed, showering me with praise. He mentioned that he would show my work to manufacturers at an upcoming amusement-park convention, and I beamed with pride like never before. "The Bryan" ride was never realized, but that didn't matter. My dad's earnest and heartfelt validation of my creativity was one of the greatest gifts he ever gave me.

Many years later, while I was in college and Pontchartrain Beach had just closed, my dad asked if I cared to join him for a drive and lunch. As his health had been in serious decline for quite some time, I treasured these one-on-one invitations. We drove to the desolate parking lot where the famed Zephyr was being torn down. We stood side by side as a gentle breeze brushed by, and I saw my father's weary eyes begin to well. I'd only seen my father cry twice in my entire life—at Dad-ee's funeral and when he told me that my mom had cancer. This gentle giant had actually been more affectionate and understanding of me than I had ever realized. I put my arm around his waist as my eyes filled, gave him a solid hug, and said, "Dad, I don't think I can watch this." He replied, "Me either, son." We jumped in his car and drove along Lakeshore Drive, ending at Masson's Beach House for a bite. I never set foot in that parking lot again.

Bryan

The cousins—David, Jay, Barbara Claiborne, Bryan, and Harry III—at Jay and Andree's home, 2016. In Jay's Beach bar, a toast was raised to the legacy of their loving grandparents, with a drink called Gratitude.

My grandfather passed away when I was fourteen. It made the TV news and the front page of the paper. He was always special to me, but this really opened my young eyes to the indelible impact Harry Batt, Sr., made in the New Orleans community and the worldwide amusement-park industry. He was a force, he was an original, and there will never be anyone quite like him. He lived his life to the fullest. How fitting that he died after an evening of dancing with Mom-ee in the ballroom of the Peninsula Hong Kong hotel.

Bryan

Opposite: John at the iconic Carousel, 1976.

Chapter 3

You'll Love the Thrilling Rides

Thrills—it's tricky. For a ride to be successful, it should not be so frightening that the desire to repeat becomes lost. In other words, don't go too heavy on the mustard.

Harry Batt, Sr., 1974

Pontchartrain Beach had multiple draws—swimming, shows, contests— but the stunning technology, beauty, and allure of world-class rides were undoubtedly Harry's passion. He had a deep admiration for the device designers, artists, and builders and a brilliant understanding of all of the subtle elements that elevate an attraction from ordinary to extraordinary. The rides that were installed at the Beach were one or first of a kind, and they towered over others in this way. His lifelong policy of the Beach having the most modern acquisitions took him around the world in pursuit of the finest talent, artistry, and cutting-edge advances.

Most of the technological headway in rides was not driven by the entertainment business but rather were spectacular progressions in aerospace, architecture, and engineering that were then applied to the industry. Harry's confidence in American ingenuity and his own boundless imagination perfectly matched the new technological heights that every part of American culture was reaching at the beginning of his second career. The device most aligned with Harry's identity was his signature "scenic railway," the Zephyr, built where there was nothing at all but boggy land and a dream. This masterpiece of a wooden rollercoaster is an ideal visual representation of his inner power and deep beliefs: where there is desire, knowledge, and craft, all things can happen. Designed by the famed Vettel engineers from Ohio and constructed in just under one year, this architectural wonder, named after the speed train Harry experienced at the Chicago World's Fair of 1933, more than established his intention to dominate in outdoor show business.

Year after year, Harry hunted throughout Asia, Europe, and the United States for the most daring and wildest designs and to make new purchases. He wasn't an "it's good enough" kind of guy. After all, this is the young man who attended a major World's Fair and returned home determined to recreate that same magic here in New Orleans. He sought the greatest value, of course, but what truly inspired him were the artistic details and visual effects of the attractions. Great attention was given to the loading stations and ride facades, many of which were designed and hand painted by Jack Ray, one of the preeminent artists in the industry. Maintaining and improving the rides each season were also priorities.

Opposite: West-end lights of the Ferris Wheel and the Paratrooper dazzled on the Midway.

The Vettel brothers were back in New Orleans in 1946 to add forty-five feet of wood to the Zephyr's outride once it was deemed a bit too scary at the first turn.

The city's heat and humidity took a toll on the rides, especially the Zephyr, and maintenance was required all winter long. New timber, fresh coats of paint, and all repairs were completed before the first signs of spring; about half of the wood on the Zephyr had to be replaced every year. Then the safety tests, first with sandbags and later with family members, commenced. Some years, the few movable rides were replaced with something new, the themed facades were updated, and rides were renamed to mirror the trends of the day.

We've written this chapter as we recall the Midway in our day, hoping to treat the reader to a day at the Beach. Imagine yourself on a sweltering summer night surrounded by the sounds of the clattering rollercoaster, the clank of the safety bar dropping on the Ferris Wheel, and the squeals and laughter from children of all ages. The 1950s might have been the boom years when attendance soared and the 1970s the peak with over fifty rides and attractions, but for Harry Batt, Sr., each decade held its own promise and sentimental joy.

The Ferris Wheel, with the creepy Haunted House keeping watch.

It was part of our New Orleans culture ... like a neighborhood backyard.
Angela Walker Enoch

No amusement park is complete without a Ferris wheel. Called a pleasure wheel in Europe and dating back to the seventeenth century, this nostalgic device is a universal starter ride, with just enough thrill to charm all ages. The Beach Ferris Wheel, at seventy-five feet high, offered breathtaking views of the city and lake. Heat lightning in a calm summer sky and squeals of happiness on the Midway were all the more enchanting from this spectacular vantage point.

Once, after eating at the Bali Ha'i in 1969, my future wife and I decided to stroll down the Midway. As we approached, a gentleman said he had just serviced the Ferris Wheel to get it ready for the park's opening. He then said, "Hey, would y'all like a free ride?" We accepted. How nice was that!

What a sweet memory. Imagine being with the one you love at Pontchartrain Beach, being the only couple on the Ferris Wheel, seeing the moonlight reflecting on the lake from the top of the Ferris Wheel. It doesn't get much better than that!
Barney M. Seely

Up, up, and away, 1946.

Make Me Smile

Pontchartrain Beach is where my enchantment with amusement parks began. It was so much more than a destination. It was a magical place filled with hope, possibilities, and romance galore. It was an emotion; it was a feeling! Many first kisses happened on that colorful Midway. From the Sky Ride and top of the Ferris Wheel, there were breathtaking views of the cityscape. My dad loved to swing the cars. Great music filled the air at all times. Imagine a place where you were allowed to drink soda and eat junk and drive a (bumper) car way before you were old enough to get a license.

Life milestones were celebrated with exotic drinks and delicious food at Bali Ha'i, and on July 4th you could sail up close on the lake and watch the best fireworks show in town. The park created a safe haven for the preteen and teen scene to be left alone by adults and feel like grownups for a few hours; it bridged the generation gap. Whenever I need a smile, I visit the Beach in my imagination, and my heart swells with joy.

Tracey Collins
Actress

The iconic clown dominated the west end of the Midway, 1940s and '50s.

Not long after Disney World opened, my parents took us on a trip to visit it. I remember coming away thinking, "I miss Pontchartrain Beach." And I still do—even though all of my most vivid memories are of vomiting up red-colored sodas after some ride.

Michael Lewis
Author

The clown head was huge. It had a wood framework constructed by my stepfather, Alfred Willis, who was a skilled carpenter. Exterior plaster was artistically applied to a metal lath, and Harry Batt, Sr., brought in a world-famous sculptor from Paris to hand-finish the iconic clown facade. Located near the west end of the Midway, it was attached to the Cockeyed Circus attraction. During the summer months, Alfred was the esteemed captain of the lifeguards.

Frank Jones

I remember the Mirror Maze, Magic Carpet, and a bunch of other crazy fun rooms in the Cockeyed Circus. One of those rooms had powerful jets of air coming out of holes in the floor, and if you happened to be wearing a skirt, watch out. That skirt would fly straight up over your head. Keep in mind that this was the fifties, and most ladies wore dresses with very full skirts. Needless to say, this room was a popular place with teenage boys!

Vicki Erwin

A direct-mail piece, promoting Chevrolet, 1960.

In the late fifties, my aunt Betty Jensen worked for a long-gone Chevrolet dealership. Direct-mail marketing brochures were the big thing. Photographers would find local amateur models and shoot photos at a popular location. Aunt Betty, being none too shy, ponied up my sister, Peggy, and me. The theme was summer fun and we had no trouble recruiting cousins and neighbors to recreate a trip to the Beach.

Chris Young

On Labor Day 1958, my father won a Ford Fairlane 500 in the grand end-of-season promotion at Pontchartrain Beach. He had the third ticket picked and the winner had to be present to claim the prize. He took my four-year-old sister onstage with him, leaving me and my two brothers to wait in the sand. It was the longest fifteen minutes of my life. We were so nervous that we dug a huge hole in the sand by hand. Finally, Dad was proclaimed the winner! We were all escorted to the car, which had been on display for weeks, and hung out of the windows while publicity photos were taken. Our family kept that car for years, and we all learned how to drive in it. While winning a car is a major event for any six-year-old, this win came at a very low point in our family's life because my mother, Vivian Kreider Mehrtens, died suddenly in October of 1957. Winning the car helped cheer us all up, especially my father.

Robert Mehrtens

Dark rides and funhouses play a significant role in any amusement park. Originally, both the Cockeyed Circus, attached to the grinning clown, and Laff in the Dark were walk-through attractions filled with scary surprises and creepy illusions. Multicolored lighting, a slanted room, one-way glass walls, and a terrifying recorded narrator amplified the fear factor. With technical advances after World War II, these attractions became automated rides, and the Big Clown was demolished to make way for a more current Haunted House. A two-story dilapidated Southern mansion beckoned riders into small coffin-like cars embraced by a large shrouded ghoul. The individual motorized cars followed a serpentine track that ascended to a second level, all the while passing frightening scenarios. Midway through the journey, the car would burst through the balcony doors, and suddenly the riders found themselves crossing the outside porch and howling to their friends below. At the other end, the car would start its descent through glow-in-the-dark frights, while recorded screams of terror and spine-tingling sounds blared. The house of horror, complete with a massive animated skeleton created by Blaine Kern Studios and a decaying mansard roof, made the Bates Motel seem more like the Holiday Inn.

As a little girl, I was often the third wheel when my older cousins took their steadies to the Beach. While seated between them, I noticed on occasion that smooches were stolen in the darkness. It wasn't for many years that I realized it was okay to kiss in the light.

Sue Vaccaro
Broadway Producer

Don't Stop 'Til You Get Enough

Courtship and romance sizzled on the steamy summer Midway. The thrill of the ride was a perfect opportunity to cozy up to your date. My first kiss took place in the late spring of 1976, with the strains of "Love Will Keep Us Together" and "Don't Rock the Boat" filling the humid night air. At the tender age of thirteen, with zits and hormones raging, puppy love abounded and I advanced from spin the bottle to full-on smooching in the Haunted House. Parents would deposit their kids at the main gate and miraculously, with no modern technology, packs of boys and girls would somehow meet and pair up within minutes. Laws of attraction will always find a way.

A gentleman does not kiss and tell, so all I can divulge is that my crush was a foxy blonde whom I met at Ice Breakers. Noticing that the line was short at the Haunted House, our group ventured over for our next ride. Funny how in a few formative years, the same terrifying dark rides of my childhood had become my adolescent Shangri-La. We boarded the cars in pairs, ribbing a burgeoning Romeo who was barely tall enough to meet the height requirement and his seventh-grade steady who was a good foot taller. I climbed into my car, offering my hand to "Sister Golden Hair," and we were off. The creepy skeleton with red-lit eyes chaperoned our every move, and my heart was racing, having nothing to do with monsters. I'd grown up on this ride and knew its timing inside and out. On the second level, I mustered the nerve to pull the old "yawn and stretch" as I knew time was running out. It was now or never. I planted a big smooch right on her Bonne Bell lips just as the exit doors crashed wide open. Busted! The cheering and jeering section went wild, and even wilder when she slapped me across my face. Sometimes "Love Hurts."

Bryan

Opposite: Local and regional school groups visited the park in the spring, which was the highlight of the academic year.

Spectacular lighting design and amplified sound—
it's the new look and the "in" thing.

Harry Batt, Sr., 1960

The beautifully designed Calypso, first shown at the Munich Oktoberfest in the early sixties, ushered in the era of dramatic lighting and design. These stunning new flat rides were not so much about intense thrills as they were about extravagant visuals and sound systems. The design consisted of a giant tilted revolving platform on which four alternating rotating arms held four individual cars. Sixteen colorful canopied cars spun to the latest top-forty hits with sound that rivaled major rock-and-roll bands. The Calypso lived up to its name as a modern celebration of vibrant color, music, and lights.

NEW ORLEANS

OFFICIAL MONTHLY PUBLICATION OF THE CHAMBER OF COMMERCE OF THE NEW ORLEANS AREA

The summer scene at Pontchartrain Beach
Algiers—the way it was and the way it is
Just which way are the railroads heading?

That's Pronounced Ka-Lie-O-Pee

My fondest memory of Pontchartrain Beach is when I was in elementary school. My dad, Henry Drueding, maintained the calliope that provided music for the Flying Horses Carousel. He was a pipe-organ specialist until his death in 1962. Before the park was opened for the new season, he would take me along when he readied the classic calliope each year. The workers at the Beach sure did spoil me. I had the run of the park and was allowed to ride in Kiddieland to my heart's content. It's a time I will never forget.

Elizabeth Drueding-Ours

Jane Sikes, 1972.

Top: The ever-popular Carousel, early 1970s.

Mary Louise Landry Cabiran with her daughter Cassandra Cabiran, 1953.

College coeds posing for a publicity shot.

The Carousel, fondly called the "Flying Horses" in New Orleans, was the most elegant device at the Beach. The merry-go-round was the first amusement-ride experience for many of us, and the simulated galloping and looped, turn-of-the-twentieth-century carnival music created indelible nostalgic memories. The Beach Carousel was a covered beauty with prancing hand-carved and painted stallions. It was housed in a structure featuring a hand-painted mural depicting various childhood fairytale characters. Fancy mirrors that reflected the hanging circus lights, and the calliope, an air-powered Wurlitzer pipe organ, easily made this ride one of the most beloved of all.

The Sunday Times-Picayune

DIXIE

New Orleans, June 11, 1978

Working Up a Rage!

Page 6

I loved Pontchartrain Beach. I *never* rode the Zephyr—one of my life's regrets. So I conquered my fear and did the first commercial for the Ragin' Cajun. My first acting job! When the park opened, I knew it was summer. Like the Northern Lights, the neon glow as you traveled up Elysian Fields was a glorious sight for a young kid growing up in New Orleans. I lived nearby in Pontchartrain Park, but the trip to Pontchartrain Beach was truly a trip to heaven for me.

Wendell Pierce
Actor

Will It Go Round in Circles

The Ragin' Cajun was the last major ride added to the Beach's lineup of attractions. It premiered in 1978, costing $1.3 million in disco-era dollars. To purchase this very same all-steel rollercoaster now would cost upward of $5 million. At the time, this modern marvel was one of only two steel rollercoasters not only in the South but in the entire nation that combined both 360-degree corkscrews and loops. The extreme thrill reached speeds close to fifty miles per hour and was smooth, sleek, lightning fast, and unlike anything before its time. Very few amusement parks could boast having both a steel and wooden coaster; in fact, Pontchartrain Beach had two of each—the Zephyr, Zephyr Jr., Galaxy, and Ragin' Cajun! The Ragin' Cajun moved to the Great Escape Amusement Park in New York, where it continues to thrill.

You'll Love the Thrilling Rides

Say Yes, Ask Questions Later

One fall Saturday afternoon in 1977, my dad said, "Son, come take a ride with me." It wasn't to grab a bite together, which we occasionally did on weekends during his off-season. He didn't give me a clue. He just said, "Get in the car; it will only take a few minutes." We drove to New Orleans East and stopped in front of a long line of flatbed train cars. Each car was loaded with enormous chunks of twisting white sculptural metal. We both got out of the car and stared upwards at the mysterious yet majestic sight. He smiled, put his arm around me, and said, "Son, that's the 'Ragin' Cajun!'" Reverence.

Bryan

Lost in the vortex of the first corkscrew of the Ragin' Cajun.

Opposite: Cover art for press materials announcing the magnificent Ragin' Cajun.

Rumor Has It

Urban legends and expert strategies are a humorous part of any amusement park, and the Beach had many. Ride aficionados shared tips on how to make the most of any visit, and locals repeated "true" stories generation after generation. Always eat meals two hours before even looking at the Wild Maus, sit in the first car on the Zephyr, be the first off to run to the next ride, and use the Sky Ride to get across the park were some that made good sense. However, we are not sure of the veracity of "children died inside the clown head," "you can pass the height requirement by teasing your hair or wearing platform shoes," or "the Musik Express is speedier at night when the lights blink and certain songs make it go faster." The jury is still out on whether or not the Ragin' Cajun was five times scarier when it was wet after a rainstorm.

Do the Bump!

The cars were spiffed up each decade (shown here in the 1950s) and were always a top favorite.

I was taught it wasn't nice to hit, but on the bumper cars, all bets were off.

Bryan

The bumper cars in the 1970s.

The Rainbow Connection

The Magic Rainbow was one of the rides that could be moved around on the Midway as needed, and the name changed now and then to suit the times. Passengers stood next to one another along the inside perimeter of a large circular platform. They leaned back against individual sections, and the only safety elements were a simple chain and two side handles; otherwise, the rider was completely unsecured.

The attraction rapidly spun in circles, pinning the rider back with the centrifugal force, then the revolving platform hydraulically tilted upwards to a near forty-five-degree angle. While "stuck," boys and girls would try to fight the laws of physics and pry their limbs from the backing. It was a big deal if you could turn your whole body upside down midflight!

The first major ride installed after World War II was the iconic Wild Maus. Designed in Europe by Franz Mack and constructed right on site in 1959, this terrifying single-car wooden coaster was an enormous draw and by no means was it as meek as a mouse. In fact, to this day it is regarded as one of the scariest thrill rides ever produced. The unique design featured cars that were actually wider than the track and attached only by the rear axle. These clever technical elements amplified the sensation that the car was always on the verge of flying off the tracks or that you were hanging off the sides about to plunge to the Midway. An automated chain delivered individual cars to the very top, before you were treated—or depending on how you looked at it, subjected—to several sharp 45-degree turns and a labyrinth of hair-raising dips and bunny-hop hills. The turns were tight and there was no transitional track like on a traditional coaster. A series of what seemed like 180-degree jackknife switchbacks and impressive pivots places this device in any rollercoaster hall of fame. Even for riders with nerves of steel, the Wild Maus was a test of courage. There was no middle ground; you either loved it or loathed it.

My family went to the Beach on most summer weekends. I vividly remember one visit in 1970 when my aunt Rosie, who had never been on the Wild Maus, joined us for the day. We got on and I sat in the front because I was the teenaged kid. When we reached the first turn where you felt you were going off the end, she peed her pants, and I had to walk around all day with wet pants.

Donna Dauterive

Wigged Out

In July 1969, my husband, Ken, and I spent a wonderful day of endless fun with our sons at Pontchartrain Beach. As it was popular to wear wigs at that time, I chose a short, shaggy style and added pizazz with a fancy hair ribbon. At ages six and four, the boys were too young to ride the Zephyr, so we decided to make the Wild Maus our big thrill. All aboard! Next I knew, my wig flew off on one of the insane hairpin turns and landed under the ride's structural framework. When we exited the ramp, the attendant proudly waved what seemed to be a dead animal. He was excited to reunite me with my head critter. As he handed me the wig, I thanked him and asked if he'd mind crawling back under the framework to retrieve my ribbon. Everyone watched as he retrieved my fashion statement, most trying not to laugh out loud.

After all these years we still smile when we remember the day "Mom's wig flew off on the Wild Maus."

Dees Veca

No One Puts Baby in a Corner

After World War II, the booming middle class gave birth to an all-new avenue for entertainment revenue at the Beach—Kiddieland. Device makers scrambled to create moppet-size rides and attractions designed specifically for tots. Harry designated the space around the iconic Milneburg Lighthouse for an all-new play zone for kids. In 1949, the Zephyr Jr. was completed, and the season opening was celebrated by crowning a king and queen of Kiddieland. With a circular boat ride, dual-wheeled kiddie Cadillacs, and the Smoky Mary train, park attendance skyrocketed.

Top: An aerial view of Kiddieland, 1970.
Above: Siblings Jerry and Susan Stagg perched in front of the Milneburg Lighthouse.

Everything Old Is New Again

*I*couldn't wait to be tall enough to experience the big rides with my cool teen cousins. But in the meantime, they kindly joined me as I reveled within the confines of the candy-cane fences and confectionary border of Kiddieland. I enjoyed many of the rides in the youngsters' playground—the helicopters that ascended at my command; the Zephyr Jr., which packed a wallop despite its diminutive size; and the little boats. Heaven only knows what was in that tinted blue water. The Smoky Mary, however, was my favorite. It was located next to the landmark Milneburg (often mispronounced "Mil-en-burg") Lighthouse. Old-fashioned steam-engine cars chugged along a meandering track while kids rang a bell, just to give parents that extra-special annoyance. The little engine that could climbed to the second level of the farmhouse and continued on its bumpy way. Towards the end of the seventies, the Smoky Mary was converted to Jungle Jeeps. By this time the ride did not interest me unless I was accompanying the same cousins' own small children, just as they had done with me.

Bryan

She's So Shy

I loved going to work with my dad, but I was painfully shy around the many teenagers who worked in the Games Department. One teenager was exceptionally kind. I don't know what his real name was, but my dad always called him Squirrel. If my dad liked you, he'd give you a nickname, so I'm sure Squirrel was one of his favorites. One morning, Squirrel asked me if I had played on the new Rocket Slides. I shook my head no. He said, "Give me a few minutes, and I'll make them especially fast just for you." About forty-five minutes later, he returned and said, "Now, be careful, because they're super slippery!" Whoa! This slide was slick and fast. Squirrel had rubbed the chutes with wax paper. He asked if I liked the slides and I shyly nodded yes. My thank-you wasn't overly bold, but I've always hoped he knew how much it meant to me.

Lisa Williams

Best in Show

Looking back at it, I was doubly blessed. I was able to secure a job with the paint and maintenance department during the day; after that shift ended, I showered at the bathhouse and walked to Bali Ha'i, where I bartended into the night. This was in the late sixties to mid-seventies, and both jobs were a blast. I painted the Haunted House, Wild Maus, Zephyr, and most of Kiddieland. One time the boss came out with what looked like a thousand paintbrushes. The whole crew was going to paint the Flying Horses. We all took pride in our work and competed to see whose horse was best.

Luie Minera

In the mid-seventies, the Rocket Slides replaced the Kiddieland entrance and the Red Baron replaced the Helicopter Ride. Floating above the throngs was the graceful, calming Sky Ride.

Siblings Vangie and Billy Schmidt (front) and friends take a spin on the Ladybug, early 1980s.

Left to right: Ramsey Schmitz, Melissa Murray, Gerard Schmitz, early 1980s.

A popup of cousins, early 1980s. Left to right: Gerard Schmitz, Stephanie Murray, Melissa Murray (middle top), Jessica Jacobson (middle bottom), Whitney Cole, Jeremy Jacobson, Ramsey Schmitz (far right).

The ride's operator looks on as future WTIX radio personality Bob Walker (boy in backseat) sails away with his friends, 1950s. It's Mommy's day out for his aunts, the Compagno sisters, and his mother, Grace C. Walker (far right).

Right: Jonathan Mares (left) and Richard Cyr on the high seas, 1983.

It is generally accepted that without a flume ride, you're not in the fun-park big league.
Harry Batt, Sr., 1970

Wet-N-Wild

The log ride burst onto the amusement scene in the 1960s and by the mid-1970s was a status symbol of any major park. These attractions consisted of hollowed-out "logs," which floated in fiberglass waterways and were based on the old "mill rides" and "chute-the-chute" rides made popular in the dawn of the twentieth century. However, the worldwide splashing sensation was not fully perfected until Karl Bacon of Arrow Development applied hydrodynamic technology, which helped make the modern-day log ride what it is today. The Beach's Log Flume was introduced in the 1970s, and its watery tunnels and big dip quickly became a favorite attraction, not only because of the innate fun but because it was a surefire way to get wet and cool down in the scorching heat of a New Orleans summer day.

Nearer My God to Thee

As a small child, I was frightened by any ride where my legs dangled outside of the car. Oddly enough, I adored the terrifying Zephyr and Wild Maus, but the benign Ferris Wheel, breezy Paratrooper, and mellow Sky Ride were a no-go. The reason for my intense phobia harks back to an early-spring day when my older brother, Jay, and I went out to the park to test the new rides, something we often did before opening day. For the Sky Ride test, we took our places on the painted yellow circles, the conveyor car scooped us up, the safety bar was quickly lowered, and we were up, up, and away. At the very tip top, we came to a grinding halt and I took an immediate dislike to my predicament. While I tried to remain calm, my ever-compassionate brother started to make the car bounce as he shouted out phrases one only heard in a seventies disaster movie. Next thing I saw was two firetrucks, sirens blaring, racing down the vacant Midway and stopping miles below my dangling feet. The fire ladder slowly cranked upwards, extending all the way to our car, and I really started to lose it at the thought of peeling myself out of the car in midair without a net! I was a blubbering mess, while Jay sarcastically recited the Twenty-Third Psalm—"yea, though I walk through the valley of the shadow of death"—which he had recently learned in Catechism. Just as the ladder reached us, a gentleman emerged with a big camera, and there was a series of flashes and rapid-fire camera clicking. It took every bit of courage I had to muster a smile given the circumstances, but I guess it's instinctual for me to pose for the camera. As it turns out, the whole thing was a publicity event to show the safety of the new Sky Ride, and everyone knew this but me. I must have missed the memo.

Bryan

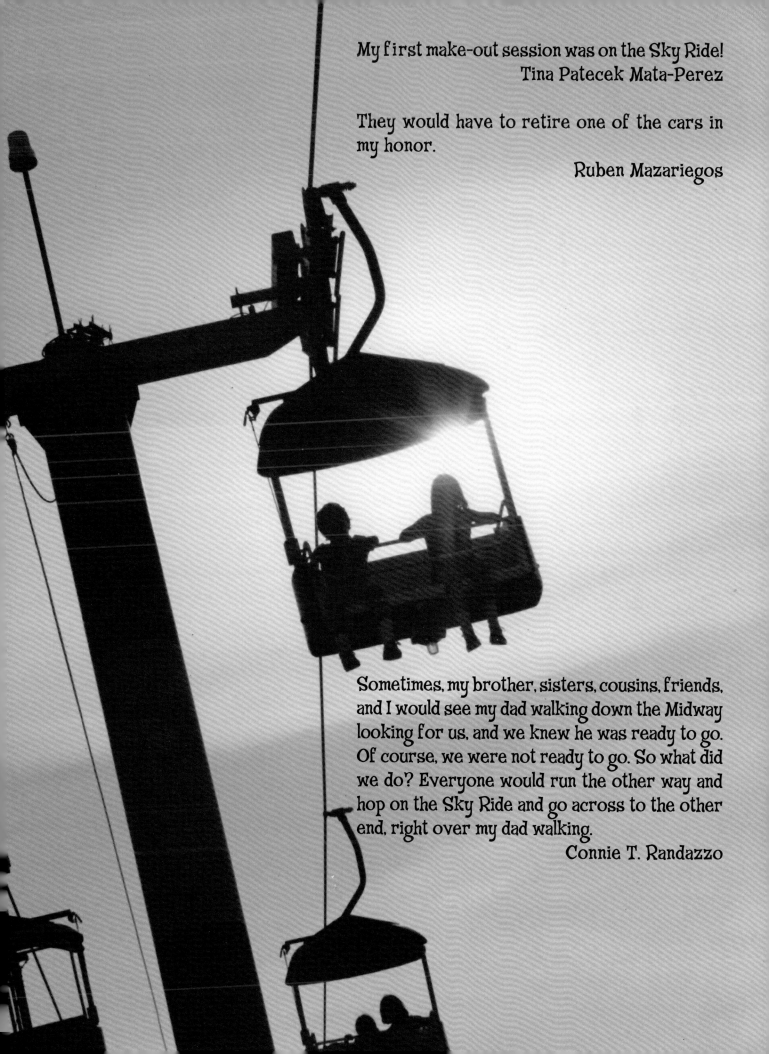

My first make-out session was on the Sky Ride!
Tina Patecek Mata-Perez

They would have to retire one of the cars in my honor.

Ruben Mazariegos

Sometimes, my brother, sisters, cousins, friends, and I would see my dad walking down the Midway looking for us, and we knew he was ready to go. Of course, we were not ready to go. So what did we do? Everyone would run the other way and hop on the Sky Ride and go across to the other end, right over my dad walking.

Connie T. Randazzo

The Bug holds the esteemed honor of being the one and only ride that moved from the Spanish Fort location and remained in operation until the final days of the Beach. Like a loyal best friend, the Bug was part of Harry Batt, Sr.'s career from day one until the closing. Created by the American engineer and early rollercoaster designer Harry Traver, the Bug was the perfect mix of thrills for just about everyone, making it immensely popular and extremely lucrative. Like a wacky centipede, buggy cars rapidly traversed hills and valleys on a circular track. There was not much to hold on to and the loud buzzing sound amplified the thrill. We can't imagine how it would pass safety codes today. At maximum speed, that first hump was a doozy. You may have barely known the person seated by your side at the start, but trust us, you were quite familiar by the end.

The Bug was my first ride where I experienced that "stomach left up in the air" feeling. I was terrified—and so young . . . wanted the ride to end but then couldn't get enough of it!
Kim Perry Meyer

Sisters Celeste and Kathy Landry holding hands in front of the Bug, 1950s.

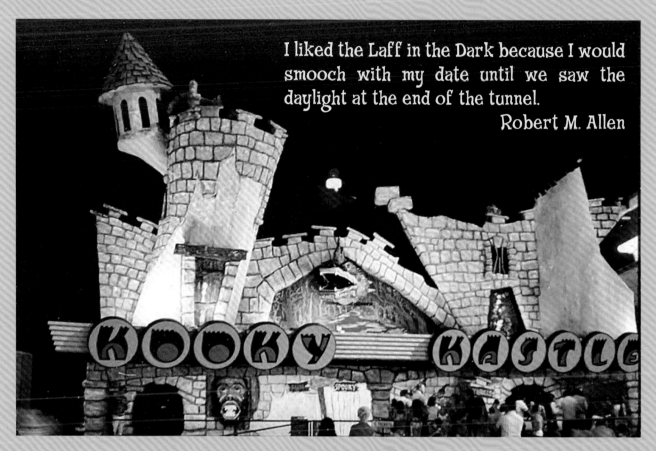

I liked the Laff in the Dark because I would smooch with my date until we saw the daylight at the end of the tunnel.

Robert M. Allen

Creep Show

Towards the east end of the Midway, near the Bug and the Shooting Gallery, was Laff in the Dark, a dark walk-through attraction that was relocated from the original Spanish Fort site. Post-World War II, it morphed into a creepy automated dark ride named the Kooky Kastle and was further altered in the seventies as the Whacky Shack. The aesthetic for both was weird rather than frightening. The TV hit *The Twilight Zone* comes to mind as potential inspiration.

A true story: One day, at Pontchartrain Beach, my father and I were just walking from one ride to the next. My father noticed smoke billowing out the back of the Whacky Shack. He let go of my hand and jumped the turnstiles. Dad forced the doors open on the ride and once he got in, he began yelling, *"Fire, fire, everyone get out!"* And sure enough, there was a fire on the ride. He got everyone out of the ride in time. That night he was interviewed by the local paper and was featured, with a small photograph, in an article — "Man saves people on ride" or something like that. I was very proud of him.

J. Scott Bond

Rollercoasters were always the kings of the ride business; even the great theme parks had to bow to the king.

Harry Batt, Sr., 1974

It was fantastic to get to the top of the Zephyr and see nothing but cow pasture as far as you could see.

Harry Batt, Jr., 1939

My fondest memory of Pontchartrain Beach, which I went to often, is when my older cousin, Terry, gave me the lowdown on how to kiss a girl. We were standing in front of one of the rollercoasters. He gave me a step-by-step plan . . . and, for those interested, it worked!

Harry Connick, Jr.
Musician

In 1939, Pontchartrain Beach opened at its new location at the head of Elysian Fields, and New Orleans was introduced to one of the finest custom wooden rollercoasters in the world—the Zephyr. Designed in Dayton, Ohio by Erwin and Edward Vettel of the famed National Amusement Device Company, the rollercoaster instantly became an iconic amusement-park beacon and beloved thrill ride for generations. The art-deco train was christened in the streamlined loading station by Miss New Orleans Irene Schoenberger on opening day. In typical Harry Batt style, no expense was spared and the original cost was a whopping $100,000, an enormous sum in its day. To build a similar rollercoaster today would be several million dollars! Not to mention insurance. Besides being a state-of-the-art architectural and engineering marvel, what set the Zephyr apart was the unprecedented twisting in the tracks of the first dip and the record sixty-mph speed. Wooden rollercoasters are extremely noisy and provide a "rickety" sensation as the trains fly along their tracks, which adds to the psychological fear factor. A true white-knuckle experience! There was no fence-sitting with the Zephyr.

I rode the Zephyr for my first time when I was in third grade. Being a Catholic schoolgirl, I was saying an Act of Contrition on the way up that hill. I can still hear that chain clacking!

Mary Palazzolo Bordelon

Speaking of thrills, insurance companies rate the Zephyr safer than climbing a ladder or stepping out of a bathtub.

Harry Batt, Sr.

The first time that I rode the Zephyr, I remember waiting in line when an older man passing by asked me if I was really going to ride this rollercoaster. He warned me that I would surely lose my gizzard if I did.

Antoinette Bonvillian

I'm sorry to say that the bathroom always smelled like vomit. I remember girls running in there after riding the Zephyr.

Pam Georges Dongieux

Top: Construction begins on the art-deco loading station in 1938.
Above: Well dressed, locked, and loaded, 1950s.

When I was a kid, the top of the Zephyr was the highest point in New Orleans, and right before you went down the first drop, you could see all the way to the downtown Hibernia Bank building. One time, right before the last turn, my aunt Nettie's wig flew off, and we never did find it. My uncle Sidney said some bird must be living in a twenty-five-dollar nest!

Ricky Graham
Actor

I had such wonderful escapes from the stress of school, life, and finding myself, riding the rollercoaster at Pontchartrain Beach, the Zephyr. I never outgrew the Zephyr.

Rex Reed
Writer

One day I rode the Zephyr fifty times in a row with my friends Robin Grisoli and Cindy Hufft. We were in the front seat each time.

Barbara

The Zephyr was a rite of passage. You knew you were growing up when you graduated from Kiddieland to the "Big Zephyr." On that day, you were no longer a baby.

Mo Brennan McConnell

My first memory of Pontchartrain Beach was living in a small white house right under the Zephyr. Part of the house was supported structurally by the rollercoaster itself. On Sundays, as the family had dinner, the whole house shook when the Zephyr thundered down the big hill. Everything would rattle. Peas bounced out of the bowl onto the table. We would hear and feel the Zephyr zipping over the house all day long.

David Batt

PLEASE READ
THE 'ZEPHYR' IS A HIGH SPEED 'ROLLER COASTER' RIDE. THIS RIDE IS NOT FOR EVERYONE. PEOPLE WITH BACK PROBLEMS, HIGH BLOOD PRESSURE, OR HEART CONDITIONS, SHOULD NOT RIDE THE 'ZEPHYR'. EVERY PRECAUTION HAS BEEN TAKEN FOR YOUR SAFETY, BUT IF YOU HAVE ANY OF THE ABOVE CONDITIONS, WE SUGGEST YOU DO NOT RIDE THIS RIDE.
pontchartrain beach

Anticipation

I grew up in Bunkie, Louisiana—population plus or minus five thousand. Native New Orleanians may not realize what the city and its destinations look like to kids from small towns in Central Louisiana. I would liken them to Oz and the Emerald City. We visited the Beach on several occasions in the early 1970s. My mother's siblings were teenagers and they escorted me around the Midway to all the amazing attractions that shook, twisted, flew, and frightened. A stark memory I recall is my first time in the line at the Zephyr. I failed to meet the height requirements. The teenagers sent me to wait in the hot Louisiana sun while they jumped on a car and started that infamous climb. I pouted and cried while awaiting their return. They came off the ride looking like they had taken a trip to heaven. The following year, I was shocked and thrilled when I met the height requirement and was finally allowed my first trip on the wooden goddess. The anticipation that built over a year has seared every second on that first ride into my being. I wasn't afraid at all as we crested the top. I was finally there. Thank you, thank you. Few things in life I remember so vividly.

Peter Parrino

Rock of Ages

My husband, Ken Kolb, proposed to me on Monkey Hill in Audubon Park, and of course, I said yes. I then wondered where he would find the appropriate spot to give me my ring. I knew it was coming, but I had no idea where the presentation would take place.

It was summer and so we went to Pontchartrain Beach. Ken was good at the arcade game Skee-Ball and was renowned for winning stuffed animals. I don't recall any animals that night, but we played a few other games and we probably rode through the Haunted House. Then it was on to the Zephyr.

We boarded, adjusted the safety bar, and then slowly made our way to the first peak. There was always a brief pause at the top. So, it was there, poised before the headlong descent, that Ken decided to open the blue box and give me my ring. I took a quick look and popped it in my mouth, sticking my tongue through it. And we went scooting up and down for what seemed like the longest Zephyr ride in history. Finally, we stopped, lifted the safety bar, and I could reach that ring—still safely with my tongue through it. Bliss! An appropriately romantic New Orleans proposal. And no lost jewelry!

Carolyn "Pani" Kolb

Rocket Man

During the fall and winter months, when Mom needed a break from the boys, Dad would often take us crabbing on the piers that stretched out into the lake. For an extra-special treat, he would allow us to play "Speed Racer" and drive the golf carts up and down the deserted Midway. It was odd and weirdly fascinating, even a little bit creepy, to explore an amusement park in hibernation. Just a matter of weeks earlier, the same exact spot had been fully ablaze with garish colors by day and a million twinkling lights by night. In the eerie stillness and quiet space, there were so many hidden attractions with all new meaning. The abandoned bathhouse, used for storage in the off-season, and the darkened dark rides lit only by my flashlight gave my treks a "Scooby-Doo"-like feel. When I was about ten, I thought of myself as quite an expert tree climber, so scaling the rickety catwalk to the very top of the Zephyr seemed like a more than attainable goal. I was an astronaut. I was John Glenn skillfully making my way to the highest peak of the lunar mountain. Halfway up and fully lost in my own imagination, I suddenly was jolted back to earth by the bellows of my rightfully furious father. "Dammit, son, have you lost your mind? Get your ass down here *now!*" You can't argue with Mission Control.

Bryan

One of my favorite summer jobs at the Beach was spinning forty-fives at the Musik Express. The deejay booth was miniscule with only a single tiny fan for ventilation. Needless to say the heat was unbearable, but on the flipside, my knowledge of pop hits is pretty awesome. In addition, the centrifugal force created by the speed and circular motion caused the riders to become incredibly close, which gave way to a new meaning of S.O.B.—slide over, baby!

Jay

We Will Rock You

The Musik Express hails from Germany and is loosely based on the concept of the popular Caterpillar rides. The attraction is made up of twenty cars that accommodate one to three passengers each, connected in a circular design and rotating forwards and backwards at a velocity of up to twelve revolutions per minute. Manually controlled by a microphoned operator, the speed can increase, decrease, or reverse through verbal contact with the riders. Loud pop music is supplied by a deejay in the control booth spinning the latest hits. Mention the Beach, and people immediately recall what songs were blasting in their day. Colorful cutouts of both male and female dancers, combined with a multitude of vibrant lighting effects, completed the psychedelic feel.

The Songs That Bring Us Back
"Long Cool Woman in a Black Dress"
"Don't Rock the Boat"
"Sherry"
"Winchester Cathedral"
"Last Dance"
"Free Ride"
"Crocodile Rock"
"We Are Family"
"Happy Together"
"Sugar Sugar"
"Surfin' USA"
"Brown Eyed Girl"
"Le Freak"
"Love Rollercoaster"
"All Night Long"
"Slow Ride"

After World War II, America stood in awe of aerospace engineering and the astonishing advances in technology. When the Eyerly Aircraft Company in Oregon developed devices for pilots to use in training, it didn't take long before the popularity of simulating "real" flying by controlling a plane's movements with a rudder spilled over into the amusements industry. Fly-O-Planes and later Rock-O-Planes, patented rides, were instant hits on the Midway, and soon Eyerly was manufacturing far more aircrafts for parks than for flight school.

Jack Lengsfield, a World War II airman, and Carol Hanrich photographed riding the Fly-O-Plane in 1946.

High Flying, Adored

Sometimes my dad would invite our family friends, the Hoffmans, to join us. All of their kids were older than me but made sure to include me in everything so I wouldn't get bored when we weren't in Kiddieland. There were some really awesome airplanes on swings that would go high in the air on the arms of the ride and the planes would glide out and tilt sideways slightly. I was terrified of them at five years old and was bound and determined not to get on the ride. The oldest of the Hoffman siblings, Chris (a.k.a. "Foots"), was a teenager at the time and begged me to ride with him, promising he'd take care of me—so I did. I was scared to death, but he held me tight while we flew and I felt so big and brave! When you're five years old and you look up at those plane-swings, they truly look like they are as high as a real plane. I vividly remember asking him, "What if the chains break and we go flying off?!" and he responded, "It's no problem; I can land the plane, I promise." I apparently trusted him completely!

Lisa Gerhardt Williams

The navy meets the air force on the airplane ride post-World War II.

Like a suspended merry-go-round, the YoYo provided a fanciful flight thirty feet in the air at a fifteen-degree angle. Each flying swing is simply a dangling chair sporting a strap and a bar and not much else; the ride's feeling of freedom and flight makes it irresistible to all ages. Versions of flying rides date back as early as 1908, but it was in 1972 that the portable unit we think of today debuted in Germany. The YoYo at the Beach was made by Chance Manufacturing Company, a family business based in Kansas, and installed in 1974. The spare design and brilliant lighting make this one of those rides that is thrilling and beautiful at the same time, especially at night.

My sister and I worked at the Beach one summer. I got heatstroke and passed out while operating the YoYo ride way down at the east end of the Midway. It took the managers awhile to find me passed out by my ride controls, the riders left hanging in the air. When I came to, there was a lot of barf and angry riders. Good times!

Babs Matthews

The Rotor, which relied on centrifugal force to slam whirling riders against the wall while the floor dropped out beneath them, arrived at Pontchartrain Beach in 1963.

Crazy fun! Enjoyed it until someone shared their meal.

Julie Ledet McGarry

It pinched me something bad when the floor came up.

Phylis Callais

Great ride indeed! I used to pray nobody would hurl!

Warren Montet

I always rode it as a kid. Now, I would have to think twice!

Laura Bordenave

It is on my Puke Mobile list!

Louise Buras Doell

And you just hoped no one upwind of you got sick because it splattered the next four to five people who were plastered against the sides!

Marieth Johnson

Opposite: The ever-popular YoYo, 1970s.

Pontchartrain Beach

25 YEARS OF FUN

—Photos by Van Horn.

Chapter 4
Step Right Up

The Pontchartrain Beach Midway, the spine of the amusement park, was a beloved magical and imaginative escape from everyday life in the city. Anchored by the Ferris Wheel on the west end and the Zephyr on the east, its energy was palpable. Everything about it—the lights, sounds, smells, and excitement—was part of a shared immersive experience with an enduring identity. It never fails. Ask any New Orleanian of a certain age if they remember the Beach, and you will elicit a string of fond and very similar responses—the Wild Maus, the Haunted House, that scary fortuneteller in the arcade, a first kiss, pay one price tickets, the jingle "at the Beach, at the Beach." Few things in a town this diverse retain such an intense collective bond.

In many ways, the Midway was a microcosm of the cultural and social mores of the day, reflective of the trends and desires of each generation. In good years, a few hours at the Beach mirrored the prosperous times, and in lean years, a visit to the Beach was a much-needed diversion. Either way, the beloved Midway relied on heavy doses of fantasy, romance, and thrills and the continuous ability to meet the recreational needs and whims of an ever-changing society. Harry Batt, a consummate entertainer with exacting standards, possessed an uncanny knack for knowing just what changes were in the wind and how to best deliver the latest and greatest in the world of outdoor show business. By its very nature, the Beach had to regularly reinvent itself in order to dazzle New Orleanians, and Harry loved this facet of the business most.

In order to produce a memorable family-fun experience on the Midway, Harry believed that every detail mattered. He lived on the premises and was involved in every aspect of the park, from design to music to staff morale. Nothing got past his discerning eye. Early midways, which Harry traveled the world to study, were called "amusement zones" or the Gayway and appealed to all the senses. Harry's attention to innovative ideas and drive for excellence ensured that the Pontchartrain Beach Midway did not disappoint. He hired the best lighting engineers in the country to color-wash the devices in incandescent neon hues and to accent each ride with lighting strips that fully enhanced the thrills. Thirty-five thousand feet of neon lights illuminated the Midway, making it the largest neon installation in the South in its day. State-of-the-art sound systems pumped the summer soundtrack throughout the park, making even standing in line for an attraction exciting. And every year, bright new signage enhanced every loading station, and world-renowned artists routinely updated the facades of each attraction.

Every season saw the introduction of the latest arcade games, novel concessions, and popular prizes. Early games of chance and skill, such as

Crossbow Shoot and Balloon and Darts, gave way to mechanical pay-for-play Baffle Ball tables and finally to electric pinball machines with all the bells and whistles. Servicemen on furlough or budding Romeos would show off their marksmanship to win a stuffed animal for their girls. Prizes directly reflected the changing times, offering something for every age and want: a small colorful toy for the Duck Pond, a basket of groceries during wartime at the Tango Game, or the highly coveted prize in 1940 for the Most Chic Easter Hat—nylon hose, a new invention. In 1956, as putt-putt golf became the latest rage, the Beach installed one of the finest miniature championship golf courses in the country—"Around the World in 18 Holes," named after the popular movie of the same year. And the park food was constantly updated. Famous since the beginning for its frozen custard, the Beach was the first place in New Orleans to offer soft-serve ice cream, as well as rotisserie chicken, when those innovative machines were introduced.

The Midway was beautified all year long. During the off-season, every ride got a fresh coat of paint, new landscaping was planted, and bright new flags and banners were installed. Whereas some family-owned parks might be down-at-the-heel at times or worn around the edges, the Beach always glistened. Twenty year-round employees booked acts for the summer, planned the endless promotions, and stocked the restaurants and storerooms. In season, the staff swelled to over three hundred people. Employees were treated like family, which meant they worked hard—really hard. Teachers and grandparents, both known to be good with kids, received visible positions, and teenagers provided the muscle and stamina the work demanded. Excellent performance was rewarded with the guarantee of the coveted job year after year. Many local policemen, firemen, and jacks of all trades moonlighted during the summer, and everyone focused on safety and superb service. Many employees recall the Batt mantra, "a customer is often wrong, but a guest is always right," and Harry's relentless quest to keep the Midway spotless.

Capturing the essence of optimism, vitality, and fresh wholesome spirit of the Midway in words is almost impossible. A list of the rides and attractions hardly does it justice. Before there were malls or megastores with formulaic interactive entertainment, there was the Midway with its unique personality, where people from all walks of life actually did participate and engage. Our collective emotion, therefore, is better served by looking at the many nostalgic mementos that bring us right back to a day at the Beach. Snapshots from Flag Day for Boy Scouts, a high-school class trip, or a first concert without parents are fragments of youthful promise. A staff shirt packed away in an attic, a pay one price bracelet taped to a scrapbook, and a strip of photomaton pictures quickly conjure up wistful memories of childhood fun. Long before selfies, video, and digital everything, a photo snapped at the staged saloon, an arcade recording of your voice, or a stamped coin were thrilling souvenirs. So if the mere mention of a Beach burger with fried onions or the quick phrase "meet me at the clown head" brings you back to sweet summer days on the Midway, it doesn't get much better than that.

Harry Jr. (in sunglasses) and colleagues grabbing a bite and a brew at the Ship Ahoy.

I would pray to the Blessed Mary statue in our backyard when I was young that my parents would take me to the Beach.

Mark Romig

My father literally worked every day. He owned a bar. But come summer, he would take off Monday evenings so he could drive us from Algiers to Pontchartrain Beach. We would always look towards Chalmette to see if it was raining before we left. It was a long haul back then. We always convinced him it would certainly be dry by the time we arrived. My father died when I was sixteen. Those warm wonderful Monday nights, when he gave up his only night off for his kids, never fail to make me smile and appreciate him all the more!

Tina Lae

Teens on the Midway in 1966.

I'll always remember the P.O.P. (pay one price) sticker on the back of my hand and the string clip around my wrist. We were free to spend the day and night at Pontchartrain Beach alone or with friends. The Beach was the first time I held hands with a girl and walked from one end of the park to the other. One always remembers the first time holding hands with someone you liked.

J. Scott Bond

There was only one way my parents could get us to leave peacefully: the promise of a giant soft-serve ice cream on the way out the gate.

Mo Brennan McConnell

World War II servicemen enjoying well-deserved leisure time, 1940s.

Opposite: A 1960 advertisement featuring the Zephyr.

Pontchartrain Beach was home for me. It was my first chance to really flirt with boys! Later, it was the security of my first summer job and the friendships I made there.
Lisa Gerhardt Williams

In the late seventies, the deco look seemed dated, so several rides and attractions received makeovers evoking a more "turn-of-the-century" old-fashioned feel that was gaining popularity.

The Beach was my childhood playground for the summer. My mom didn't work back then, and we went at least three times a week. We either went with my dad on the weekend or grandparents in the evening for rides and the Midway games! Such wonderful memories. I can still smell the hot dogs and my favorite—hamburgers!

Marianne Brisset

Genie Kennon Fleishel (left) with her sister, Melanie, and her mom, Suzanne, 1970s.

Tod Smith, president of WWL-TV, with his sister, Leslie Smith Everage, and their niece, Tiffany Smith Williams, 1970s.

Bob Kennon holding his toddler, Suzanne, as her sisters look on.

Bryan strolling on the Midway.

A 1970s advertisement for family fun.

$2.10 an hour and all the girls you can meet.

David Workman

I worked at the Beach in 1963 and 1964. I was sixteen years old at the time and big for my age, so I lied to get the job. I was a junior at Cor Jesu High School, and although my parents were hardworking people, the only way I could attend college was to pay for it myself. So I told Mr. Lupo (he loved smoking big smelly cigars) that I was eighteen.

I worked seven days per week, twelve hours a day, on every single ride. It does not sound like much, but I made seventy-five cents an hour, and that paid for my college tuition at Louisiana State University at New Orleans.

Charlie Tobelman

I spent two summers, '79 and '80, in the Games Department. I worked practically every game but mostly the weight-guessing booth. The thing about it was the prizes cost less than the cost to play the game, so the house always won.

Russell Vaughan

Employees sporting their staff shirts, 1970s.

Life Lessons

Vanessa Kenon at work, 1970s.

Working at Pontchartrain Beach for three springs and summers in the early seventies served as a big turning point in my life as well as the lives of many other young people in New Orleans. For many of the teens from my neighborhood, it was the first opportunity to mingle with college students, and those jobs helped to pay for graduation and prom expenses they would not otherwise be able to afford. The jobs also offered students the opportunity to pay for their college tuition. The mix of cultural experiences while meeting new friends was life changing for many of the young workers.

My fondest memories are cool breezes of the mornings and evenings rolling off Lake Pontchartrain and the laughter and running of kids at noon when the gates opened. Early-morning and late-night walks on the beach just off the boardwalk were the best of times. I also learned at a very young age a lot about the importance of good customer service, strong character traits, comprehensive and detailed training for staff, and strong safety for your customers. Respect and care for those issues have served me so well in my career in management. It all started with my first part-time job at Pontchartrain Beach. The sounds of top-forty songs from the seventies always trigger the smells, sounds, and laughter from the Beach boardwalk.

Vanessa Hammler Kenon

I worked the Carousel or what we called the Flying Horses. My job was to operate the ride and watch for the safety of small children and pregnant mothers and for what we called "jumpers"—young men who would jump onto the outside of the ride, while it was in motion.

Edwin Fleischmann

Edwin Fleischmann in his staff shirt with his mom, Emily Jaeger, near his home in Gentilly, 1957.

An aerial view of the Midway's east end, 1970s.

Rows and Flows of Angel Hair

The concessions sold at Pontchartrain Beach owe a lot to the 1904 Louisiana Purchase Exposition, a.k.a. the St. Louis World's Fair. The fair saw the invention of the ice cream cone as well as the popular introduction of hot dogs, hamburgers, yellow mustard, iced tea, Dr. Pepper, and cotton candy. Selling over sixty-eight thousand boxes at twenty-five cents apiece (nearly half the price of admission), cotton candy, then known as fairy floss, made a particularly lasting impression. The original machine-spun confection was invented by John C. Wharton and William Morrison, a dentist, in 1897. The name cotton candy emerged in 1921 when a new patent was filed by New Orleans' own Josef Lascaux, also a dentist. The process of making cotton candy remained the same until 1949, when Gold Medal Products introduced spring-loaded bases, and they have manufactured nearly all machines in production today. National Cotton Candy Day is celebrated on December 7.

Pet peeves: Careless picnickers who toss bottles, throw sand or who fail to place their rubbish in receptacles provided.

Harry Batt, Sr., 1950

Please Feed the Animals

Harry Batt, Sr., expected the park to be immaculate at all times, and it was. When Walt Disney visited the Beach in the fifties, he marveled at this and wanted the new Disney Theme Park being planned for Florida to follow suit. In 1964, Harry conceived of and developed the vacuum-like machines that would suck garbage right from your hand, and he placed them inside colorful animal figures. This was a huge success and the paper eaters were marketed to every park and zoo in the country. Kids would literally hunt for garbage just to activate the machine! Besides being fun, this kept the park clean and reduced janitorial expenses to boot. For many kids, this was as exciting as the main attractions!

Some of my earliest childhood memories are of Pontchartrain Beach. My favorite memory was how the number five became my favorite number. I was around four years old, and I remember bugging my dad until he let me play this one arcade game. I can't recall the name of it, but I remember it was a big spinning cage with numbers. The young man working the game would spin the cage and hand you a ball. You picked a number and threw the ball in, and if it landed on your number, you won a big stuffed animal. I played, I picked the number five, and I won. I'll never forget how happy I felt that night; it was the first time I had ever won anything, and as of then I had a favorite number!

Markee Berthelot

The penny arcade in the early 1940s.

My grandmother was like Mae West with red hair. She wasn't used to babysitting, so we took a cab to Pontchartrain Beach. I rode some rides while she watched, and she was wonderful about it, but I figured she was bored. I knew she liked to gamble and play the horses, so we found a mechanical horserace game and played it all night until the Beach closed. It was a dime a game, and we spent thirty dollars in dimes playing. We had a blast, won two huge stuffed dogs, and we didn't have enough money left to take a cab home so we caught the bus, which was also a dime, with our two huge stuffed dogs. Everyone on the bus loved us!

Steven Forster, Photographer

Just like in the Haunted House, I was terrified of any red light hidden in the photo booth. But I loved my souvenir cap and didn't take it off for weeks.

Suzanne Danos, 1969

pontchart beach

AMUSEME

Over 50 Thrilling Rides

Super

A full day entertainn —the bigge around! Brin whole family stay all day. R all the rides as a as you want, and see all the shows for one low *One Price* es of FREE parki

air- ases ough Plenty

ath tak- rills and rn. wild. All fun!

Added Attraction...
Free Circus Acts
For Park Patrons!
uring Regular Season)

This is my best friend, Loa Borchert (right), and me in 1975. I can still remember the way it smelled.

Stacy Ogier Hancock

My future wife, Joan Wallace, and me. This photo was taken May 2, 1969, and we were married in the next year. We are still married today.

Barney M. Seely

My sister Susan and I worked every summer at the Beach from 1972 to 1976. I worked the Duck Booth, Paratrooper, and my favorite, the Musik Express. I was also a cashier at the Ship Ahoy. It was a great place to work as a teen!
Donna Dupree Soileau

My sixty-three-year Treme pal, Larry Floyd, and me. We were in the Boy Scouts together and joined the Navy Reserve in high school (1961). Our recruiter said that women go crazy over sailors, but he was wrong; we didn't have any takers.
Jimmy Anselmo
Nightclub Owner

any Shady
cnic Areas

ere's plenty to do and see for
eryone—from tode   ens-
grandparents. Th
have fun!

Mystifying
Merlin Rainbow
be Mystifying Merlin
Magic Show. He
believable
before

Our first real date was at the Beach (1963)! We've been married fifty-four years.
Ken and Pat Parr Lanier

We're a
—an
Par
fr

through late May
hrough Labor Day.
ht on weekdays, and
urdays and Sundays.

ailable
or exact dates.)

My very last romper.
Bryan

We used to store our bag lunches in the bottom of the lighthouse, which was in Kiddieland, and the Beachcomber Restaurant offered a hot plate lunch for staff at a reasonable price. Once a year, the owners hosted a big employee party there with great food and lots of beer. It was eventually discontinued, and the rumor was that a few of the employees were dropping the beer over the open wall of the restaurant to the ground outside for future consumption.

We enjoyed seeing people going in and out of the Bali Ha'i, which was next to the Beachcomber. To a young man like me, the high-end tiki restaurant looked like the most festive and elegant place to be.

Edwin Fleischmann

Colorful neon lights illuminated the food and beverage stations throughout the Midway, 1960s.

There were three main people in charge at all times. One was given half of the Midway, another had the other half, and the third had the log ride and the Zephyr corridor. My dad, Al Stumpf, was one of them. I remember that Burnell Maxon was another. They were schoolteachers during the off-season. I loved the employee parties; they gave us painted quarters to play any arcade game we wanted! Those were great times.

Marie Stumpf

You Ought to Be in Pictures

Long before there were selfies and a camera in every person's hand, photos of fun days out with friends were far less common, if not rare. Film was expensive and largely reserved for formal family portraits. Having your picture made on the staged saloon set at the Beach during the forties and fifties was considered the epitome of cool and quite the treat. Courting young adults, bachelors out on the town, and just-married couples smiled for the camera for a souvenir of youthful summer nights.

Harry Batt, Jr., Fay Vilac, Richard Batt, Jr., Joan Boudousquie, Lois Langhoff, John Batt, Alberta (last name not legible), and Buddy Kleinpeter, July 1946.

Norbert and Frank Anglada, early 1950s.

Dudley Louis Cabiran and Mary Louise Landry Cabiran, 1948. This was their first date, and they've been married ever since.

Josie Mistretta Wehl and
Anthony Wehl.

Mayble Benoit Seely (left) and Josephine Reid Seely.

Steve and Jerry Carra.

Sweethearts on the Midway.

Manny Elwell, Harwood Styron, Melvin Collins, Martin Collins, Raymond Collins, 1946.

Anita Pelias Georges (third from left), surrounded by friends, early 1950s.

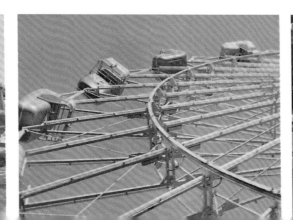

The Zephyr Jr.

I lived on the 5900 block of Franklin Avenue. We could see the fireworks and hear the crowds when the wind was blowing just right! Every time I see searchlights in the sky, I think of the Beach.
Necha Otillio Murphy

I loved to watch the heat lightning at night over the lake and those soft summer breezes.
Dianne Weber

Pontchartrain Beach was the first location in the city to present a fireworks extravaganza. Park patrons, boaters on the lake, teens on hoods of cars, and families on their roofs could all partake in viewing this spectacular free entertainment in the summer.

Cats keep watch over the Wild Maus on a space-inspired neon-lit Midway, 1960s.

You Gotta Get a Gimmick

As a kid, my favorite Midway game was Go Fish. The boy in me loved the splashing of the bobbing painted fish and the opportunity to make a mess. Best of all, everyone was a winner. But as the tween years approached, I lost interest in the Midway games, with the exception of Skee-Ball. Many a hot humid night, I waited for Dad to drive me home after closing. The air-conditioned comfort of the Penny Arcade became my "cool" hangout. I'd hit up the Fortune Teller, the Gunfighter, and of course the pinball machines. The cashiers were allowed to give us quarters to keep us occupied. But the currency was special. Dad had them painted red for me and blue for Jaybird. At the end of each night, the money counters would pull our quarters to the side so that we were well funded for the next visit. Every season, we would try to master the new games. My secret favorite that I became quite the expert at was the Stripper. Projected up on a screen a few feet in front of the joystick (oh the irony) was a seventies babe in a plunging halter top, hot pants, and go-go boots. A red dot, as a target, moved around her curves and if you hit the target, oops, she would lose another piece of clothing. Rather than taking careful aim, I would click as fast and as furiously as my eleven-year-old heart desired—rapid fire 'til she was commando. For a fleeting moment, I was hailed as "The Stripper Kid" among the arcade set, until my mother got wind of my shenanigans and the game was replaced. Looking back, I can't believe it was ever part of the gaming lineup. It was certainly a departure from the Beach's wholesome family fun.

Bryan

Chapter 5
That's Entertainment

Pontchartrain Beach was known for its brilliant parade of free entertainment. There were two shows nightly most weekends from 1938 until 1983, when Fats Domino played on closing night. Long before television or such a thing as a reality show, the Beach was the premier spot in the city to actually see a dazzling array of world-class performers. It was a big deal. The entertainment was live, it was real, and it was the best in the outdoor show business. For many New Orleanians, the free music, comedy acts, and displays of death-defying artistic skill were their only glimpse of talent from outside of the city, and the seasonal lineup was truly a gift to the community.

The nautical-themed Main Stage had a state-of-the-art sound system and was unparalleled for the vast range of shows presented. Every dancer, acrobat, and trapeze artist, and later every singer, musician, and band, wanted to play the Beach. Although the types of shows and style of performers evolved over the decades as tastes in popular culture changed, one thing remained consistent—Harry's entire roster of shows was family friendly. There were no tawdry acts, sideshows, or human oddities at Pontchartrain Beach. Riveted by the discipline and athleticism of the biggest names in the country, he booked act after act of aerial cyclists, daredevils, and tightrope walkers. Delighted audiences streamed into the park summer after summer, packing the Midway and lining the seawall in eager anticipation of the eye-popping performances. There wasn't a bad seat in the house.

The late thirties through the fifties were the heyday of circus acts at the Beach. During this golden age, aerialists, acrobats, and high-wire dancers astonished the crowds with their stunning feats of mental prowess and physical strength. Harry brought the best troupes to town, hoping to inspire local spectators to reach for imaginative new heights in their own lives. It may seem quaint now, in a time when almost nothing is novel or breathtaking, but before television, these displays of remarkable talent were a source of great national pride and a definite morale boost in tough times. The Flying Wallendas, the famous family of high-wire daredevils, offered a glimpse into another world as their stunts pushed past the normal limits of balance and agility. The Skylarks, the Great Rollini, and Kurtz and Kurtzo stunned the crowds with enthralling contortions in the air and on poles and trampolines. Such feats of skill and visual art were thrilling beyond measure and fired the imaginations of spectators of all ages.

Opposite: Excitement builds for the nightly free show on the Midway, 1950s.

As television and the movies made their way into more and more homes in the fifties and sixties, circus acts such as the Henderson Juggling Trio or Walter Jennier and his trained seal, Buddy, fell out of fashion. These charming acts were replaced with baby-boom-friendly productions designed specifically for the rapidly growing new entertainment market—children and teenagers. For kids and their parents, Merlin the Magician, porpoises Skipper and Dolly, and musical revues filled with song and dance provided rousing belly laughs. Showy antics and zany stunts, such as marriage on a high wire, the human cannonball, and the electrifying high diver through a ring of fire, amused a wide range of ages. But the hungriest new consumer by far was definitely the teen. Music—it was all about music—and the Beach outdid itself in this arena.

Beginning in the fifties and continuing through the seventies, band after band performed on the Midway. Emerging artists, local luminaries, and musical legends of all kinds played at Pontchartrain Beach, making it hands down the coolest place in town. The concerts, often with accompanying themed dances, more than appealed to the booming teenage culture afoot in the city, and the free shows were packed. Everything about the Midway appealed to the teen scene. The first tastes of freedom, budding romances, and live hip music brought the third generation of Beach patrons to the lakefront in droves. To top it all off, from 1955 to 1963, the local radio station WTIX partnered with the Batts to host a wildly popular Appreciation Night at the end of every summer. Thousands of patrons turned out for free rides, autographs, and the exhilarating lineup of musical stars.

In 1955, the Beach hosted popular local disc jockey Red Smith's second annual Hillbilly Jamboree, with Elvis Presley billed as the top act right along with the Miss Hillbilly Dumplin' beauty pageant. In the late summer of that year, he was a regional sensation for sure, but he was not the star that he would soon become once his number-one smash hit record, "Heartbreak Hotel," was released in early 1956. When he returned to the Beach the next summer, he was the leading figure of rock and roll and his mere presence on the Midway sent park patrons swooning. Little did Elvis nor Harry Batt, Sr., know that when their paths would once again cross, it would be on a world stage—the Seattle World's Fair—but that's getting way ahead of the story. Elvis's two visits to the Beach are legendary in New Orleans summer history.

Top: The boat-themed Main Stage, in the center of the
Midway across from Bali Ha'i and the Ship Ahoy.

Betty and Benny Fox, the famed Sky Dancers, promoting their upcoming Beach season by performing at the top of the Roosevelt Hotel, 1940s.

The Flying La Vans, 1920s.

Hanging from the Family Tree

In recent conversations about our family's amusement park and our grandparents, it was unanimously determined that my cousin David and my brother, Jay, most embodied aspects of Harry Sr., and my cousin Barbara those of Marguerite. I guess that leaves Harry III and myself as somewhat of a mix. Like all families, we have a little bit of our grandparents and parents in our faces, hearts, and souls, and I'm just fine with that. Among so many attributes, the one thing I grew to admire most about Dad-ee is that he never wanted to stop learning and trying new things. He experienced life to the fullest. I would like to think that some of that spirit and joie de vivre live in me, which is maybe why writing this book has inspired me, at my somewhat advanced age, to take trapeze lessons from aerialist Lorelei Ashe. No joke, yesterday I actually hung from my ankles!

Bryan

Harry "Pops" La Van (center, pointing up) and Harry Batt, Sr. (second from left), talking to trapeze artists at the Beach, 1930s.

Jack Dempsey (above left) saved autographed photos from just about every act that performed at the Beach. This picture (above right) is from one of his many scrapbooks.

My father, R. J. "Jack" Dempsey, was the emcee for the Beach's stage and circus acts for many years. His full-time job was police reporter for the *States-Item*. He was a big Irishman with a booming voice, which made him perfect for the Midway. My two brothers, sister, and I spent many summer evenings there, riding with Dad from our Mid-City home out to the lakefront. There were two shows every night. My favorite one was of the "Nerveless Nocks," a family of four who swayed atop the highest poles we ever saw out on the sand, changing poles as they bent over! As soon as the first show was over, we would run over to the main office with Dad to pick up our special tickets to the rides. We got to ride everything once. The Batts were a very generous, gracious family. In our eyes, our dad had the perfect part-time job!

Colleen Dempsey Carmichael

25 TH. ANNI...

Gay Midway

Rides to thrill the young—and the young-in-heart. Fun-filled amusements provide a wholesome good time for all the family.

KIDDIELAND

Jet Fighter to thrill air-minded youngsters. Jr. Zephyr for real roller coaster fun. Kiddie Boats, Pony Cart, Roto-Whip and other gay rides for tremendous fun.

Free Parking—Free Admission

Never a charge for these free services. Courteous people to help you park. Friendly folks to help make your visit more enjoyable.

THRILLING FR...
"NATIONS TOP...

The ...

Dazzling Thrill-a-Ba... one minute and la...

The SK...

Twin High Sway give you the shiver

SHOWS AT 7:30-11:0...

EXTRA PERFORMAN...

25 YEARS OF FUN

Our silver anniversary marks an important milestone in the history of Pontch... five years of providing fun and recreation for the people of New Orleans and its... enjoyable for us.

Your continued support has been most gratifying in our efforts to make Ponte... to which New Orleans may point with pride. Only through continued service, and... ward providing the finest in facilities and recreation can we merit that support.

Pontchartrain Beach, as long as we are connected with its management, will ce... nity asset worthy of the highest traditions of our industry and our city.

We thank you,

—HARRY J. BATT, President

PONTCHARTRA...

Skipper and Dolly with their trainer, late 1960s.

Lisa Gerhardt Williams and the dolphin trainer, 1960s.

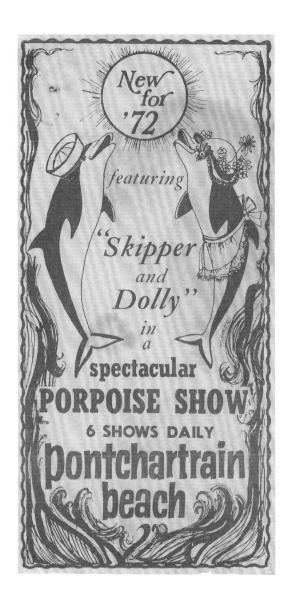

Hello, Dolly!

One of my dad's favorite things about working at the Beach was the porpoise show with Skipper and Dolly. He watched the rehearsals and got to know the trainers. One weekend, he arranged for me to be one of the kids chosen for audience participation. He even hired a photographer to memorialize the event. I got a special nautical-themed dress for the pictures, and when the trainer, Theresa, asked for volunteers, I raised my hand as planned. She selected me along with another little boy. She explained how the porpoises instinctively helped struggling swimmers and asked us if we wanted to take a swim with them. I had seen the show and knew what was up, but the boy excitedly took off his shoes and grasped her hand as she counted down to dive-in: "One . . . two . . . thr—okay, I'm just kidding!" He was so disappointed. Instead, we called, "Here, Dolly!" and Dolly the porpoise jumped out of the water and up onto the side of the pool, where we knelt down to pet her while Theresa fed her fish. It was such a special time! My dad was not a very outwardly sentimental person, but he framed his favorite photograph and it hung on our living-room wall until he passed away.

Lisa Gerhardt Williams

The Flaming Cannonball was a highlight of the daily diving show.

The diving shows were amazing. I was dazzled by the artistry in motion, the soaring, flipping, and twisting through the air . . . the incredible physiques. I secretly and desperately wanted to be a diver, but Speedos were just not for me

Bryan

Allen Gagnet dives from a thirty-foot platform in 1977.

The comical Aquamaniacs entertain the crowds in 1977.

Gemini Space Twins waiting to be shot from space-themed cannons, early 1960s.

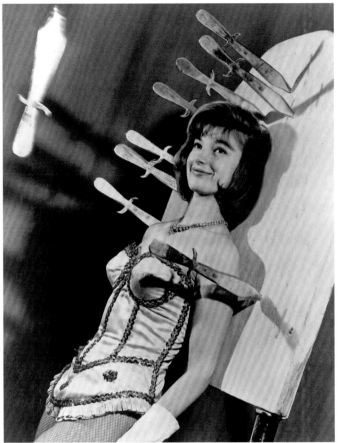

Elizabeth Collins, 1966.

Part of my duties was to go over to what I called the Beach House to assist with the animal acts. The Beach House itself served as the dressing room and green room for the various performers. I remember the elephant and chimpanzee acts specifically. For the elephant acts, I assisted with moving the platforms on which the elephants would climb to do their slow-motion acrobatics. One evening, as I was walking through the Beach House, one of the chimpanzees, who was sitting on a stool near the walkway, grabbed my hand and bit me. Although it didn't hurt, it definitely got my attention.

Edwin Fleischmann

Beatrice Dante and Peanuts, 1959

I sweated inside the Merlin suit so much that I began to have repetitive dreams that my feet were being cut off, but it was just my toes separating in spasms caused by a lack of potassium.

Lisa Roach Maddox

Lisa Roach Maddox, as Merlin Rainbow, with her assistant, Claudia Vasilovic, 1970s.

A contact sheet of the Merlin Rainbow Show for promotional materials, 1970s.

A contact sheet of rides and the Summertime Spectacular revue, 1970s.

Our band, the Singles, had played many of the live music clubs like Jimmy's, Jed's, and many CYO dances, but playing the Beach was amazing. The concert was sponsored by a local radio station and many of the city's new wave, rock, and soul bands were on the lineup. I had a feeling that Mr. Batt may have had something to do with our invitation, but he never let on. What a great day.

Dr. Charles (Chuck) V. Menendez

The Singles, 1982: Steve Lafasso, Chuck Menendez, Dave Claret, Bryan Batt, Charlie Weinman (not pictured)

Pontchartrain Beach was a great place to bring a date. You had no choice but to sit super close to each other (actually touching!) on the rides, and when you were in junior high, that was pretty thrilling. The Bali Ha'i seemed like the coolest place in the world, and a place that only adults could hang out in. My fondest memory was when my old high school band, Lik (terrible name), played on the big stage that Elvis had once played on. I remember that we asked our lead singer to not wear his stupid Mickey Mouse T-shirt onstage. He wore it anyway so we kicked him out. Once upon a time the coolest place in New Orleans.

Vance DeGeneres
Producer

The Summertime Spectacular revue, 1970s.

Harry Batt III with Morgus the Magnificent, a New Orleans icon, 1950s.

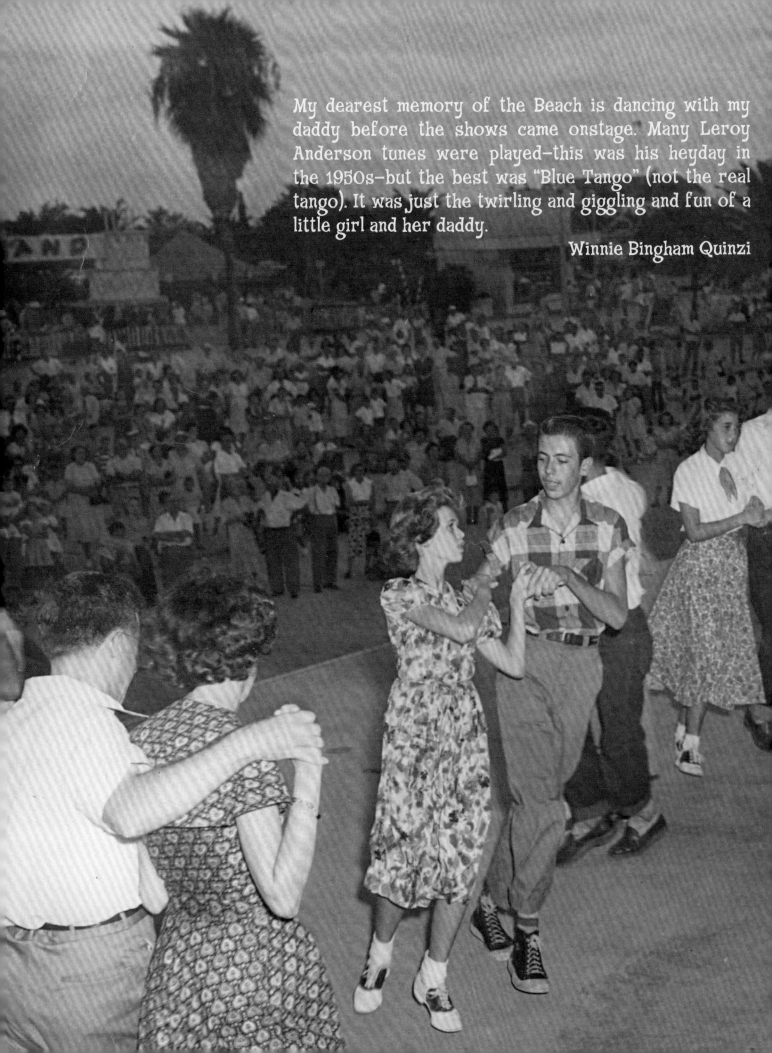

My dearest memory of the Beach is dancing with my daddy before the shows came onstage. Many Leroy Anderson tunes were played–this was his heyday in the 1950s–but the best was "Blue Tango" (not the real tango). It was just the twirling and giggling and fun of a little girl and her daddy.

Winnie Bingham Quinzi

It was like a whole different world. You left your troubles behind and just had fun! My grandparents lived by Audubon Park and would pick me up in the very early fifties just to walk the Midway and get a snoball or ice cream. It was an evening out when we may not have had TV yet; families made their own programs together!

Margaret Connolly Delery

A preshow square dance in front of the Main Stage, 1950s.

Our biggest problem at the Beach first is that young people don't think of their own safety. We have to watch out for them. Next came their behavior and their morals. All have been our responsibility and I think we've met it.
Harry Batt, Sr., 1970

Johnny Crawford

Roy Orbison

I saw the Animals perform, or try to perform, on the Beach stage. They were cursing, then all of a sudden there was no sound. Security came onstage and informed them that if they couldn't perform without cursing they wouldn't be allowed to continue! Times sure were different.
Ruth Babin

I remember seeing Frankie Avalon perform and at one point our eyes met. I thought I was going to have a heart attack.
Donna Rae Conner

Fabian

Mac Rebennack, a.k.a. Dr. John,
performing in the early 1960s.

I have many memories of Pontchartrain Beach. The first thing that comes to my mind is that playing there was very near to my spirit. I was taking guitar lessons from Roy Montrell at the time, but I played the gig on multiple instruments. I remember playing bass there. I remember playing guitar there, too. I conducted my band at the WTIX Bandstand. Charlie Miller played trumpet—he played with the Bucktown Horns—and he was my partner from my earliest memories. I'll never forget the gig playing with the Beach Boys at Pontchartrain Beach—I backed 'em up. Pontchartrain Beach was 100 percent one of the best times of my life.

Dr. John
Musician

"At the beach, at the beach, at Pontchartrain Beach, you'll have fun. . . ." I'll never forget Jimmy Buffett serenading Bryan and me with the Beach's theme song at the opening of my new restaurant Tableau. If you grew up in New Orleans (or on the Gulf Coast like Jimmy) in the seventies, the mere mention of Pontchartrain Beach brings back a flood of great memories.

Dickie Brennan
Restaurateur

That's Entertainment

Kelso On Republicans   Should We Shut Down The Dome?

FIGARO

FREE

May 5, 1976   Published Weekly In New Orleans   Newsstand Edition   25 Cents

Summer In The City

A Special 12-Page Guide On How To Survive The Hot Months In New Orleans: Music Schedules, Sno-balls, Pontchartrain Beach, Summer School Guide, All About Ceiling Fans, Swimming Pools, Much More!

Elvis Presley At Pontchartrain Beach, Summer Of '55

I have a hunch about this Elvis kid.
Harry Batt, Sr., 1955

Harry Batt, Sr., and Elvis Presley with local beauties on the Beach stage, 1955.

Robin Sher and Elvis on the Midway, 1956.

Let Me Be Your Teddy Bear

My mom met Elvis at Pontchartrain Beach on her twelfth birthday in 1956. He was on the Midway throwing baseballs to knock over bottles, and he gave his winning prizes to my mom and her younger sister. Mom still has one of those prized kewpie dolls that Elvis gave her, which survived Katrina's floodwaters, however a bit worse for the wear. She also had an autograph, but I'm not sure if it survived.

Dewey Scandurro

Elvis with his girlfriend, June Juanico, at the Beach in 1956.

All Shook Up

A few months after Elvis performed on the Beach stage, his first big hit, "Hound Dog," became a national sensation. Needless to say, there was quite a buzz when the word got out that he was visiting New Orleans again the following year. Harry Sr. planned a big dinner party at Ship Ahoy to welcome him back to the Beach. Uncle Johnny and Aunt Gayle extended invitations to the whole family. We were all so excited; we had been fortunate to attend many fun events at the park, but this was truly amazing. As always, there was an abundance of Polynesian food and drink and fried chicken, per the King's request. Everything was splendid. Then midway through the evening Elvis cracked a tooth on an hors d'oeuvre.

Donna Mackenroth Cole

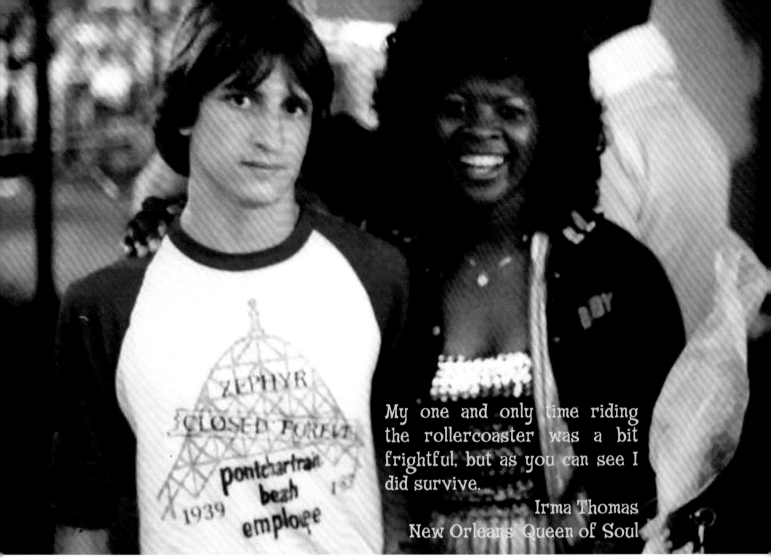

My one and only time riding the rollercoaster was a bit frightful, but as you can see I did survive.

Irma Thomas
New Orleans' Queen of Soul

Mike Perry and Irma Thomas, early 1980s.

Working at the Beach was one of the landmark times of my life. While in high school, I spent my summers working in all departments but mostly in guest relations, the heartbeat of the whole operation.

One of the most fun days was working a beer stand at the foot of the Main Stage, while artists such as Irma Thomas, Iron Butterfly, and Fats Domino performed. I was an aspiring drummer, so I timed my break in order to sneak up onstage and sit behind the drummer from Iron Butterfly while he played "In-A-Gadda-Da-Vida." Wow, what an experience! I was thrilled to meet Frankie Ford, Miss Irma, and Fats, all of whom were incredibly gracious and friendly. It was one of my first experiences rubbing elbows with "New Orleans Music Royalty" and they couldn't have been more down to earth. Many years later, I ran into Irma Thomas at the Voodoo Fest and she was still as sweet now as she was then. Pontchartrain Beach etched some wonderful, lasting memories into my life.

Michael Perry

Pontchartrain Beach closed after Labor Day weekend in 1983. A few weeks later on September 24, the Beach hosted a star-studded fundraiser billed as "The Last Ride," to benefit the Contemporary Arts Center. The CAC was founded in 1976 and the Batt family supported their many educational and family-centered public programs from the very beginning. Fats Domino was among the performers at the final show on the famed Beach stage. Singing his hit song from 1960, "Walking to New Orleans," was a perfect finale to a perfect evening.

Chapter 6
Beauty and the Beach

With a steadfast commitment to the continued development of the lakefront land that he leased from the Levee Board, Harry consistently made capital improvements at the Beach, maximizing its recreational value. By the time he opened at the new location, swimming for exercise, rather than simply for bathing, was all the rage, and sun tanning was thought to have endless health benefits. With that in mind, a state-of-the-art bathhouse was built in 1941. This Art Deco masterpiece included every modern convenience. In 1948, he was instrumental in expanding the beach, making it the largest manmade beach in the world in its day. By 1957, an all-new boat dock extended 1,000 feet out into the lake as the departure point for a fifty-person sightseeing boat and prime docking for private motor and sailboats.

The Beach's shore glistened, and lifeguards, in the pre-liability days, patrolled the sands providing trained supervision. Families fleeing the heat in summer months flocked to the Beach with picnic baskets in hand. Parking was complimentary, and colorful umbrellas, towels, and even swimsuits could be rented. Many a city child received free swim lessons at what Harry called the Beach Swim Club. It cannot be overstated how much this beautifully maintained beach contributed to the park's enormous success. And Harry, as always, remained on high alert for ways to expand any beach-related attractions.

In 1921, the first competition of women on parade in bathing suits was created in Atlantic City. It was a clever attempt to extend the summer season—and therefore, revenues—past Labor Day, the traditional closing weekend. This uniquely American invention, billed as a "beauty tournament," was an immediate and resounding success. Contestants came from all across the Eastern Seaboard, the audience actively participated in voting by clapping for their favorite girl, and a trophy was handed to the competitor who exuded the most "fitness, vigor and good health." This early pageant morphed into the Miss America Pageant, which launched a bevy of spinoff and feeder pageants across the country. And because the concept originated at a beach, for decades the women naturally were crowned in their fashionable bathing suits.

Of course, Harry jumped on this idea, and with the nation's ever-increasing fascination with Hollywood glamor, he was quite confident that Pontchartrain Beach would discover the most eager and talented contestants. He hosted the very first Miss New Orleans pageant at Pontchartrain Beach in 1930. Dorothy Dell Goff, a local young singer with promising radio contracts, was

Opposite: A bathing beauty takes center stage, late 1940s.

Lawrence Landry, Gordon Willhoft, Myra Willhoft, Arlin Batia, and Isabell Landry building sandcastles.

crowned the winner. She moved on to New York City, where she performed on Broadway in the Ziegfeld Follies, and then to Hollywood, where she signed with Paramount Pictures. His 1931 Miss New Orleans, Dorothy Lamour, an aspiring actress, went on to become a movie star, most known for making the sarong famous in *The Jungle Princess*. In 1933, the next talented Miss New Orleans, Louise Schmaltz, won the Miss America title at a pageant held at the Chicago World's Fair. Pageants were by now considered to be a route to stardom, and like Harry, New Orleanian contestants had big dreams.

By 1935, when Mary Healy won the title of Miss New Orleans and began a fifty-year career in show business, the Pontchartrain Beach stage was considered to be one of the greatest steppingstones in the country for aspiring actresses, singers, and dancers. Tied into movies and wanderlust, with known agents scouring the many pageants, the Gayway was now the Gateway to stardom. Both local and national businesses flooded the Beach with advertisements, and in poured swimsuit company sponsorships. Pageants meant that parents, grandparents, and entire neighborhoods streamed in as spectators, and park attendance spiked with every event.

Harry had an uncanny aptitude for the soaring pageant industry. Pre-television, these contests were billed as exciting and charming stellar performances. When Irene Schoenberger was crowned Miss New Orleans in 1939 at the opening of the new location, an astounding 50,000 people cheered her on, breaking all attendance records to date. During World War II, Harry considered dropping the competitions, but the morale boost for the entire city was deemed too beneficial. Instead, he marched forward with citywide participation, wartime themes, and prizes such as a $1,000 war bond for the Beautiful Legs contest, sponsored by the national company Venida Hosiery. It was pure genius.

Once the war ended, the beauty-pageant craze boomed just like babies and the movies. Glamorous Hollywood-inspired gowns were introduced to the competition, and in the fifties scholarships were added. Harry brainstormed an array of fun contests covering a myriad of themes and holidays. There were Little Miss Sunbeam, Junior, Senior, and Mrs. titles, Best Easter Outfit, and Twins Day. Neighborhood establishments got involved in supporting their own Miss Bywater or Miss Gentilly. With the finest department stores in

the South, such as Maison Blanche and D. H. Holmes, and the most prominent businesses, such as Chevrolet, providing fashion, prizes, and cash awards, the competitions became an engaging and beloved part of the fabric of the city.

Tapping into the country's fascination with all things Hollywood, the Beach also coordinated with films being premiered at the Joy or Saenger theatres by staging movie-star lookalike contests and hosting cast appearances. Local celebrities acted as emcees and anyone wishing to compete simply had to show up in costume. Before television and the Internet, if you wanted to see an exciting live show, you headed to the Beach. It seemed that the entire community rallied around each and every event. It was pure show business!

At its peak, the Beach hosted ten official pageants a season and endless themed contests. In 1958, the Beach crowned Arlene Howell as Miss Louisiana before sending her on to become Miss USA and a runner-up at the Miss Universe pageant, and in 1961, the pageant did the same for Sharon Brown. Once the Miss America pageant was televised, the era of live Beach pageants slowly declined and would never be the same quaint, homespun entity. Many a career was launched at the Beach before the last pageants were held there in 1967.

Top: Artwork from the twenty-fifth anniversary brochure.

There's a great galaxy of beauty at the Beach with an array of charm and talent to rival any Broadway stage or Hollywood screen.

Harry Batt, Sr., 1950

I had been swimming, and a friend wanted me to enter the contest. So I got out of the water, tied my wet hair back with a ribbon, put on some shoes, and just walked down the boardwalk once. When they told me that I'd won, I couldn't believe it.

Louise Schmaltz, 1933

Matching swimsuits and sunbathers on July 4, 1946.

Pontchartrain Beach BREEZY BREVITIES

NEWSY ITEMS — PICTURES AND PERSONALS FROM NEW ORLEANS' FAVORITE PLAYSPOT

No.

SUNDAY, April 21, 1946

World Of Fun" Is 1946 Beach Theme

N'S BEST
L ACTS ON
H PROGRAM

and excitement galore
red Pontchartrain Beach
during the 1946 season
program of free acts which
'Pop" Lavan has scheduled.
wing Capt. Roy Sims, who
his first appearance at the
on Easter Sunday, will
a steady succession of new
and some of the most popular
ners of other seasons.
an is now dickering with
attractions of international
and is holding several open
for them. But his program
lists many of the top aerial
vils of this country and

them are the Great
balancing marvel who
on April 28; the popular
ks, those high pole stars
a sensational "breakaway",
begin a two weeks engage-
on May 5; Kurtz and
one of the greatest high
acts in the business, will
at the Beach on May 19;
Walter Jennier and his
ed seal, Buddy, are booked
(Continued on Page 3)

others Day Program
nned at Beach
y 12

others Day will again be ob-
ed at Pontchartrain Beach on
12 with a program that has
to be one of the most popu-
f each season.
dreds of families annually
mother out for a day at the
h, and many participate in
afternoon program during
honors and tribute are paid
and the mother with the
oldest mother, the youngest
ildren at the Beach.

DOROTHY NELL ADAM

NEW THRILLS,
MANY EVENTS
ON SEASON CARD

With "A World of Fun" as
theme and a world of activity
its program, Pontchartrain Bea
begins its first peacetime seas
in five years this Easter Sund
Throughout four years of w
Pontchartrain Beach played
prominent part in the recreati
plans of the armed forces. Ev
before war began, the Army reco
nized the Beach recreation faci
ties by establishing a large recr
tion camp at the rear of t
Beach property. Throughout t
war years, soldiers, sailors a
marines found at Pontchartra
Beach relief from their tedi
war jobs. Thousands of war wo
ers were able to do better th
after a day of healthful fun
the Beach.
Now the picture has chang
Again most of the servicemen
back in civilian clothes, and th
at peacetime production. As t
season progresses, more and m
of the wartime restrictions
transportation and goods wil
released.
Orleanians will find it m
convenient to come to the Bea
(Continued on Page 4)

Pontchartrain Beach BREEZY 'N BREVI

NEWSY ITEMS — PICTURES AND PERSONALS OF NEW ORLEANS' FAVORITE PLA

SUNDAY, JULY 21, 1946

MISS NEW ORLEANS CONTEST TOPS

PRINCESS OF BEAUTY—1946

, winner of the 1946 JUNIOR MISS NEW OR-
field of 26 young beauties at Pontchartrain.

Winner To
Opportunity
Travel, Care

No New Orleans gi
received a greater
than will fall to the win
1946 Miss New Orleans
Pontchartrain Beach, A
and 15.
Travel, education, and
for success on stage, sc
radio will be hers as she
for Atlantic City to compet
Miss America pageant.
The winner of the Miss Ne
leans contest will be comp
outfitted, given her trave
(Continued on Page 4)

Double Happiness

LINE" ON BEER PRICES
COSTS, ENTERTAINMENT

Pontchartrain Beach BREEZY BREVITI

NEWSY ITEMS · PICTURES AND PERSONALS FROM NEW ORLEANS' FAVORITE PLA

SUNDAY, MAY 26, 1946

UNE TO BE GALA MONTH AT THE BEA

Mr. New Orleans Gets Award and Smile

lane Gridiron
er Winner of
r New Orleans

Cash, 22 years old and
of muscular might,
title of 1946 Mr. New Or-
one of the most repre-
fields ever to compete
annual event at Pontchar-
Beach on May 17.
end at Notre Dame
d at Tulane in 1945—
and excellent swimmer
star weightlifter—Cash
cellent background for
velopment. As soon as
out before the judges
rge Beach crowd it was
that he was one of the
vorites.
place went to Tommy
the N.O.A.C., winner
1941 Mr. New Orleans
nd third place was awarded
A. Entz.
, Cash, also repre-
N.O.A.C., being a mem-
that club's weightlifting
unds 6 feet, 1 inch tall,
al inch chest expanded, a
waistline, 24½ inch thigh,
inch calf.

Dick Tracy F
Hunt, Flag Da
Among Events

With schools closing
weather in prospect a
gram of events has been
uled for Pontchartrain Beach
ing the month of June.
Thousands of youngster
expected to participate
Dick Tracy Funhunt,
for Saturday June 8, in co
tion with the popular Beach
program presented on Ma
through Friday over radio sta
WDSU.
(Continued on Page 5)

Star Singing Twins

1945
JUNIOR
MISS
NEW ORLEANS
WELCOMES
1946
SEASON

I was Little Miss Sunbeam from ages four to eight, representing Holsum Bakeries and their summertime promotions with the Beach. The most popular was when children could bring in a bread wrapper in exchange for an entire free day of rides! My memories remain fond to this day.

Mary Fanning Horaist

A promotional photo celebrating the pool.

Dive In

There were three swimming pools at the Beach. One was a kiddie wading pool with tables and chairs around it for adults to enjoy refreshments while watching the toddlers. One was the seventy-by-forty-foot diving pool, eight to eleven feet deep, which was the stage for death-defying diving contests from a thirty-foot platform. But the crown jewel was the ultramodern Thyra Damonte swimming pool, which was built for the 1957 season replacing an older pool. The Olympic-size pool featured a wall of metal and old sandstone decorated with artful sea fantasies. It was dedicated to the female national champion swimmer from New Orleans who captured the nation's imagination in the 1920s. Like everything at the park, this pool was in a league of its own.

Because of

HURRICANE BETSY

pontchartrain BEACH

Will Be Unable to Open

as Scheduled

SATURDAY

or

SUNDAY

Father Knows Best

In 1965 when Hurricane Betsy was bearing down on New Orleans, my mother wanted our family to wait the storm out at her mother's home on St. Charles Avenue. Dad had to remain at work and suggested that everyone hunker down in the bathhouse. He reasoned that the ridge at the lake was above sea level, higher than most of the city, and since he had witnessed the building of this fortress, he knew that Betsy was no match. Dad predicted that the huge oak branches that lined the Avenue could present a bigger problem, but Mom opted to join her extended family at my grandmother's. A few hours into the storm, towering limbs came crashing through the roof, electricity was lost, and this hurricane party quickly deteriorated into disaster. Dad was right and from then on, my mother evacuated out of town for any storm mightier than tropical. And the bathhouse? It went unscathed; however, the Ferris Wheel did take a joyride down the Midway.

Bryan

Sunshine On My Shoulders

In 1974, when I was nine, my mom had a severe heart attack, and she was hospitalized for many weeks. I spent the weekdays with my grandma, and on the weekends, my dad took me to work with him at the Beach. As the purchasing agent for all of the restaurants, my father had to be there at 5:00 A.M. to supervise the deliveries. On our way up Elysian Fields, we'd stop at Lawrence's Bakery, and I was allowed to pick out anything I wanted for breakfast. To heck with doughnuts; I went straight for petits fours and specialty cookies with chocolate milk. Once on the property, I'd grab my beach towel and head for the lake. That's where I'd have breakfast, watching the waves with the sun rising behind me, shining pink and gold on the water. I'd bring a bucket and some sand toys and spend the morning walking from one end of the shoreline to the other. I amassed quite the seashell collection. I also played with many tiny crabs and other creatures that lived in the shallow water. It was absolutely incredible to have that time alone on a beach that felt like mine and mine alone. Though I spent almost every other weekend at the Beach every summer for the next nine years, I can count on one hand the number of times I ran into anyone else walking along that section of the beach at that hour. I felt very safe. When I got tired of being on the beach, I'd bring all my things back to my dad's office in the storeroom of the Games Department and walk over to the remodeled playground area in Kiddieland. Gone were the huge birthday cake and other decorative structures, replaced by huge rocket slides, springy animals to bounce on, and big metal daisies for climbing. When the park opened at noon, I rode the rides to my heart's content until my dad left at 4:00 P.M.

Lisa Gerhardt Williams

An aerial view of a packed summer beach, Main Stage, and Kiddieland.

Beauty and the Beach

A vintage postcard from 1941 depicting the shoreline and Midway.

A great memory I have was being at the Beach with my oldest sister, Nancy, who had moved to the U.S. from Cuba just as Fidel Castro took over. We were in the sand and swimming in the lake, when all of a sudden my sister stood and called out the name "Brito." She spotted one of her friends from Cuba right there at Pontchartrain Beach. It was great to see two longtime friends from another country reunited. Neither knew the other was in New Orleans. Again, a beautiful memory I will never forget.

It was hard when Pontchartrain Beach closed, since it was such a big part of our lives. What I wouldn't give to be back on those shores again!

Elizabeth Drueding-Ours

Sunbathing and swimming in the early 1950s.

Making Waves

With the women's right to vote in 1920 came the right to wear much less cumbersome clothes, and the Jazz Age woman was bold and adventurous. For swimming, designers reinvented suits to meet the changing attitudes. Hems went higher, and part of the lifeguard's duties at the time was to monitor the crowd for decorum by measuring the distance between a woman's knee and the hem of her suit. By the thirties, sun tanning was in vogue, and tighter, stretchier fabrics, deep plunging backs, and the emergence of conservative two-pieces all meant added comfort and more skin exposure. The navel remained covered, and a short-skirted bottom concealed the upper thigh well into the fifties. Eventually, the little "modesty panels" were ditched for form-fitting glamorous shapes, much like the ball gowns of the era, and by the sixties, the teeny bikinis were here to stay.

Mary Lee Aucoin Rodriguez and friends, 1945.

Tanning in pre-sunscreen days, 1950s.

Lylia Lagarde and Carol Shoemaker posing for the Breezy Brevities, 1946.

Lestor Otilla, the grandson of Clovis Martin, the inventor of the po' boy, as a lifeguard in the early 1950s.

The FUN SPOT of the South

Promotional images from the twenty-fifth anniversary brochure.

I loved my days as a Red Cross-certified lifeguard at Pontchartrain Beach; hands down, it was probably the best summer job any young man could ever ask for. Occasionally, Harry Sr. would invite us to the Ship Ahoy for dinner, and he would say, "You know, you boys have it pretty darn good. You get to be in the sun at the beach all day, enjoy the attractions, rides, and entertainment all for free, and all in the company of beautiful young ladies in bathing suits . . . and get paid for it. Hell, you should be paying me!" And you know what? He was right!

Eddie Sapir
Former New Orleans City Councilman

Lifeguards posing before taking their posts.

Beauty and the Beach

Life Guard at Ponchartrain Beach

Frank Minyard standing near his rescue boat, mid-1940s.

Nice Work If You Can Get It

We had the privilege of interviewing Dr. Frank Minyard, former coroner for the city of New Orleans, who we learned had been a lifeguard at the Beach. He invited us to his beautiful farm on the Northshore to hear his wonderful firsthand stories. Dr. Minyard has the presence, swagger, and joie de vivre of a man more than half his age, and he is a true New Orleans gentleman and renaissance man.

As he tells it, when he was an adolescent, he was inspired by Tarzan movies and set out to emulate the jungle he-man by developing his own similar natural abilities in swimming and physical fitness. In the early spring of 1945, when he was sixteen, a fellow junior at Holy Cross recommended that this all-American blond buck apply for a lifeguard position at Pontchartrain Beach. The monster-sized captain of the lifeguards, Al Willis, put the young recruits through rigorous testing. While some of the boys were a little scared, young Frank wasn't afraid of anything. So, the head lifeguard asked, "When can you start?"

Frank explained that the job entailed great responsibility because in those days, the guards' duties were all encompassing. They were not just lifeguards but also EMTs as well as a peacekeeping mini security force. At times the young sailors from the nearby base would imbibe too heartily and become feisty and require policing. For three summers (1945, 1951, and 1952), Frank enjoyed fun in the sun while weightlifting in the guard's hut and even placed second in a Mr. New Orleans contest. Catching the Midway shows and free meals at the Garden Terrace or Ship Ahoy restaurants were all perks, but his blue eyes really sparkled as he mentioned that the best of all was clearly meeting all the bathing beauties on a daily basis.

Their entire day was spent in the direct summer sun, whether on the elevated white wooden guard's chair or on the long floating platform, which had a diving board and stretched out into the lake. This was before the swimming pools were constructed. The young men had rowboats and pirogues to rescue swimmers who ventured too far out. The guards all had great tans, and this was before sun-protection knowledge, so the lotion of choice was the classic combination of iodine mixed with olive oil and later baby oil. To beat the heat, "air conditioning was new, and I spent my days off sitting in the Saenger all day long," Frank said.

"My last summer, we decided we wanted a ten-cent raise, and I was elected to approach Mr. Batt to represent the other guards. I knocked on his door on the property at 7:00 A.M. on July Fourth. He answered the door dressed in a red silk robe with a cigar in the pocket, and after I made my case that we were underpaid, he agreed to the raise. I guess I implied that we would strike on such an important day, but we hadn't really decided that and I was dressed in my suit ready to work. It was a beautiful experience for a young Tarzan; in fact, I saved more lives as a lifeguard at Pontchartrain Beach than I ever did as a physician!"

What's Good for the Gander

At the turn of the twentieth century, displays of the male physique focused on feats of strength and endurance. But as the "fitness" contests became popular for women, men's competitions for "bodybuilding, proportion and poise" grew right along with them. Pontchartrain Beach held many Mr. New Orleans "best developed tournaments." Over the years, contestants included enlisted men, Beach lifeguards, muscle men from the New Orleans Athletic Club, and later, and Tulane and LSU athletes. By the thirties, men's swimwear no longer included shirts, and by the late forties, with Lex Barker, Hollywood's Tarzan of the Apes, at the height of his popularity, high-waisted swim briefs highlighted the masculine attributes. The 1949 Mr. New Orleans contest drew 20,000 people, proving that what's good for the goose is good for the gander.

Faye Wagner and Warren Breaux, winners of the New Orleans Athletic Club's summer fitness competition, July 26, 1955.

Tommy O'Hare (left), Mr. New Orleans 1954; Maxine O'Hare Dammon; and his brother, Jimmy, a former Mr. New Orleans.

Musclemen on the Midway: Herbert Hackley, Terrell Brunet, and Ray Simioneaux.

John Batt registers contestants. Left to right: Audrey Williams, Frances Baiamonte, Marlene Meyer, Sadie.

A beauty pageant lineup, early 1950s.

Lyla Hay Owen, Miss Bywater 1951.

Miss Bywater

Growing up, my family actually lived within walking distance of Pontchartrain Beach, and as a young girl, I remember watching the beauty pageants in awe. My father noticed "that look" in my eyes and said, "Now don't you get any ideas about entering any of these contests." I don't think he relished the idea of his little girl parading around the stage in a bathing suit. Well, several years passed, and I was bitten by the acting bug. At the encouragement of friends and my agent, I entered the Miss New Orleans contest, as they thought it would be great for exposure and publicity. Although I entered with great reservation and trepidation, the entire event was more glamorous than I could have ever imagined. What a wonderful memory!

Lyla Hay Owen
Actress

Kathy receiving a first-place trophy from actor Lex Barker, also known as Tarzan of the Apes, at a lookalike contest held at the Saenger Theatre.

Kathleen Langla, Miss New Orleans 1961, graciously met with us so we could pore over her fabulous photographs and news clippings depicting her experiences at Pontchartrain Beach. At seventy-eight, Kathy exudes timeless beauty and exuberant positivity. She has a fantastic sense of humor and a whip-sharp memory; we could have visited with her for hours.

Kathleen's entire family moved to New Orleans from New Iberia in 1957 for her father's employment opportunities. She laughed as she described "six kids in a panel truck with mattresses along the sides—country mice heading for the big city for the first time." She was seventeen and thrilled. "It was unreal," she said. "It was also the very first time that I'd seen a beach, and the lake was so vast, green, clear—you could see your feet through the water in those days."

She was a middle child responsible for her three younger brothers, "so everywhere I went, they went," she recalled with a chuckle. "We walked to the Beach from Arts Street just about every day in the summer—forty minutes each way—and were home before dark. I loved to just sit and sunbathe. The lifeguards were beautiful [more laughs] and very well mannered. Many were Tulane law or medical students so grateful to have the job. You needed pocket money for the rides, but the beach was free."

Above and opposite page top left: As Miss New Orleans, Kathleen is photographed with cadets for armed-forces promotional materials.

Dancing with Lawrence Welk at one of her many celebrity engagements.

Kathleen landed her first job as a clerk in an office on Canal Street and saw nothing but possibilities in her new hometown. She joined the Crescent City Strutters as a lead twirler and also Miss Hamilton's entertainment group, which performed for World War II veterans. Miss Hamilton was a highly regarded promoter at the time, organizing talent for advertising, fashion, and events of all kinds. Kathleen really captured our imagination as she described herself dancing and pantomiming as Elvis and lip syncing as Rosemary Clooney. She sang "Mambo Italiano" like it was yesterday. After months of Miss Hamilton's persistent nudging, she entered her first pageant, Miss New Orleans 1960.

"I didn't see myself that way; I was a late bloomer," Kathleen said. "With my knees knocking, I walked on the Beach stage in my favorite peach bathing suit, but I was the first to wear a swimsuit without that little flap in the front. That was a big deal." Kathleen was crowned first runner-up and captured the attention of the Crescent City Athletic Club, which offered her a complimentary membership, worth thirty-seven cents a day, in exchange for touting their health club at local events.

"It was all just great fun," Kathleen told us. "I made lifelong friends, girls swapped clothes, and we all did our own hair and makeup. When the 1961 pageant rolled around, I was confident in my own olive-skinned tan, pretty white bathing suit, and a beehive 'do that my friend gave me that day. It was a wonderful time, and being crowned Miss New Orleans opened so many doors for me."

Kathleen shared so many remarkable stories with us—getting keys to the city from Mayor Schiro, dancing with Lawrence Welk when he visited, and winning a Charleston dance contest on the same night that she won the Jane contest at a Tarzan appearance at the Saenger. But the story that charmed us the most is when she told us that Harry Batt, Sr., personally asked her if she still had the peach swimsuit from her first pageant, and she sure did. He wanted to shoot publicity pictures of her and that suit matched the hibiscus trees near the main entrance perfectly. Kathleen placed in the final five at the Miss Louisiana pageant held that year at the Beach and was crowned Best Personality by her peers. It is more than obvious why.

Winner of the Marilyn Monroe lookalike contest.

Miss Louisiana 1956 seated in front of the hand-painted mural in the main office.

In the years 1954, 1955, and 1956, I competed in the Junior Miss New Orleans beauty contest at Pontchartrain Beach. One of those years, I was picked ninth out of fifty girls. The announcer kept calling one of the finalist's numbers; I didn't think it was mine. As I was leaving the stage, I looked at my banner and there was the very number he was calling. Oh my! I was so excited. One year, the finalists rode in convertibles down Canal Street for a boat promotion, and that was lots of fun.

Rose Marie Roger Randall

William Randall and his future bride,
Rose Marie, on a date in 1956.

Surprised pageant winner Madelyn Burke with
Rita Sevin (left) and a friend, 1966.

Marlin Bourg Donham, 1960s beauty queen.

The world premiere of the big-budget Hollywood film Reign of Terror, *featuring Arlene Dahl as "Madelon," took place in New Orleans, and the Beach celebrated with a lookalike contest, 1949.*

The world premiere in New Orleans of the hugely popular movie Tammy and the Bachelor, *starring Debbie Reynolds, was celebrated with a "Tammy" lookalike contest at the Beach, 1957.*

An evening gown competition in 1958.

Chep Morrison, a former mayor of New Orleans, surrounded by local beauty queens.

WBOK DJ and Cajun singer Red Smith serenading Alberta Louise Futch, Miss Louisiana 1958.

Judge Gerald Gallinghouse, Sr., holding Jay as he gets a kiss from Miss Universe Iêda Maria Vargas from Brazil, 1963.

BALI HÁI
at the Beach

OVERLOOKING BEAUTIFUL PONTCHARTRAIN BEACH
NEW ORLEANS

Chapter 7

Mai Tai Madness

Bali Ha'i may call you,
Any night, any day,
In your heart, you'll hear it call you:
"Come away . . . come away."

So sings the haunting melody and unforgettable lyrics of Richard Rodgers and Oscar Hammerstein's Pulitzer Prize-winning musical based on the James Michener award-winning book, *Tales of the South Pacific,* published in 1947. With the Kon-Tiki expedition and men coming home from World War II with exotic souvenirs and stories of orange sunsets and tropical lifestyles, the romanticized version of faraway cultures was simply irresistible. The swanky tiki culture in Hollywood was on Harry Batt, Sr.'s radar as early as the late 1930s, but Polynesian pop culture did not truly explode on the American scene until the late 1940s.

When he opened Bali Ha'i, a sensuous tiki lounge and restaurant at the Beach, in 1952, he quickly captured the imagination of the New Orleans cocktail set and diners keen for an exciting and original experience. And it was. The fact that old-school, well-established, traditional French restaurants had dominated the special-occasion clientele for generations didn't even cross Harry's mind. He had never been a follower, and his confidence in his timing was unabashed. An A-framed structure covered in bamboo and a thatched roof replaced the Beach Terrace restaurant, and Bali Ha'i quickly became the most glamorous place in town. Noted set designer Josef Lenz assisted Harry in meticulously decorating the dining room and cocktail bar with hand-painted murals, Tahitian thatched huts, and rafters draped with all things South Seas inspired. The exotic ambience was swoon-worthy and simply the drive itself "out to the lake" had a seductive sense of "getting away," since many patrons were making the trek from neighborhoods throughout the city.

Bali Ha'i had a sophisticated party-dress and coat-and-tie dress code, and the lush decor and jazz-influenced island music filled the space. Waitresses in sarongs served potent libations as customers relaxed in fan-backed wicker chairs surrounded by waterfalls and flickering lanterns made from blowfish. The atmosphere was as intoxicating as were the drinks. Parents often walked into this cool paradise after settling their kids on the humid Midway for a night of safe amusement or parked in the enormous lot where the Sampan, derived from the Cantonese word for the flat river boats used in the South Asia waterways, shuttled them to the restaurant's main entrance. The fact

A watercolor by Don C. Smith captures the essence of Bali Ha'i. It virtually sings the evocative lyrics "here am I, your special island, come to me, come to me."

that the Sampan was actually a highly decorated pick-up truck bothered no one, especially after a Mai Tai or two.

As with all of his endeavors, Harry Batt, Sr., was laser-focused on every detail that would deliver an engaging experience, from menu planning, to exotic drink recipes, to designing the ceramic tiki mugs for the signature cocktail, the Fogg Cutter, which are prized souvenirs still today. Harry Batt III relayed one of the funniest stories to us that fully illustrates his grandfather's passionate personality even once he was "retired." His dad, Harry Jr., told him that at three o'clock one morning, after being home from work for only two hours, he received a phone call from Harry Sr. informing him that the fortune cookies at his dinner table that night were all "bad." After a heated exchange, Harry Jr. told Sr. that from then on he was welcome to write all of the fortunes himself. And he did.

Like in New York City and Los Angeles, the tiki craze in New Orleans was a moment in time in American culture that seems quaint now but was groundbreaking in its day. The city was ripe for the trip-to-paradise theme and a peek into distant lands, making Bali Ha'i wildly successful. The potent rum drinks served in carved-out coconuts and pineapples, the built-in babysitter, the Midway, and the uber-swell atmosphere were the perfect backdrop for a multitude of special occasions and, as such, provided enduring fond memories of a magical place.

My Island Goddess

When island visitors entered the exotic world of Bali Ha'i, Miss Laverne, the hostess with the mostest, greeted them with great flourish and style. I was mesmerized by her colorful muumuus and batik sarongs. Her Lucille Ball red hair was beehived high atop her head, crowned with an orchid or gardenia. She would shepherd me to the main dining room, but my curious six-year-old self longed to veer into the cocktail lounge. Catching a glimpse of the risqué image of the topless island beauty on the wall was my Mission Impossible. Miss Laverne was fast. She would deftly divert my attention by draping a lei around my neck and steering me to the giftshop, which she managed. I would spend hours among the ceramic tiki bowls and the jade and coral jewels. And she had an enchanting way of making me feel needed and valued as her assistant. She taught me how to greet customers and assigned me "very important" jobs. My favorite by far was spraying the colorful leis with a potent gardenia perfume—which, coincidentally, was my grandmother's favorite scent. To this day, whenever I smell Fracas perfume, I immediately think of these lovely ladies and the South Sea splendor of Bali Ha'i. Miss Laverne never made me feel like a nuisance, but when I reflect on my six-year-old Tasmanian Devil self, I realize she was the island goddess of patience. She was a beloved fixture at the Bali Ha'i for decades, but more importantly, she was my friend.

Bryan

Mai Tai

2 ounces dark rum
½ ounce orange curacao
½ ounce simple syrup
½ ounce orgeat syrup
½ ounce lime juice

Garnish with orange slice and green and red cherries. Serve over crushed ice.

A Polynesian Paradise

Soft lights . . . island music . . . delightful cocktails . . . superb cuisine . . . ample parking . . . just a quaint sampan taxi ride away!

RESERVATIONS
282-9859

BALI HA'I
at the beach
ELYSIAN FIELDS AT LAKESHORE DRIVE

OPEN DAILY
5 P.M.
EXCEPT
MONDAY

Tiki Bowl

2 ounces dark rum
1 ounce light rum
1 ounce 151 rum
2 ounces gin
1 ounce vodka
3 ounces grenadine
4 ounces orange juice
4 ounces pineapple juice
2 ounces falernum syrup

Serves approximately 6. Long straws are needed. When serving, place paper umbrellas in the straws.

I just wish I had been older and able to experience Bali Ha'i—the Polynesian theme, thatched roof, girls with flowers in their hair, cocktails served in coconuts with mermaids and little umbrellas peeking out. Everyone seemed happy, and why not? The grownups could enjoy the adult beverages and each other, knowing the kids were safe and having a blast on the rides in the park. Everybody won—especially the Batts. We all wanted to be them. To have free run in that magical amusement park—*wow!* We thought Jay and Bryan were the bomb; we still do!

In more recent years, we convinced Bryan and Jay to let us try to recapture Bali Ha'i at Café Adelaide and the Swizzle Stick Bar. We had little thatched roofs over the lamps and tiki paraphernalia everywhere. It was a silly but fun attempt to replicate a place we all loved. The best part was getting the much-sought-after recipe for the Fogg Cutter cocktail. Bali Ha'i may have been all about fun but those cocktails were serious!

Ti Martin
Restaurateur

Interior of the main dining room featuring a hand-painted mural of the South Sea Islands.

NATIVE DIVER **1.00**
(As daring as its name)
The pale milk of the coconut strengthened with a blend of light and dark Jamaican rum. Rare spices and a touch of ripe Mexican lime juice complete the creation.

RUM . . . nectar of the Polynesian gods . . . now famed through the four corners of the world as the perfect base for exotic cocktails and punches . . . to bring you the romance of the South Sea Isles.

BALI-BALI **1.00**
(The nectar of the Polynesian Gods)
The lightest of the Jamaican rums is gently combined with the finest Virgin Island rum in a chilled container. Carefully measured portions of herbs, and the aroma of Hawaiian juices, are added to complete this masterpiece in mixology.

TAHITIAN BREEZE **1.00**
(During feast time South Seas Maidens find this punch refreshing)
A deft blend of two light rums with sacred fruit juice. The flavor is completed with a touch of Louisiana Cane Juice.

BORA-BORA **1.25**
(As delightful as the Island for which it is named)
On the sands of the sun-kissed isle of Bora-Bora the natives gather in the evening to concoct and enjoy this rum-based drink which their ancestors originated centuries ago.

WAIKIKI GOLD **1.00**
(The delight of Hollywood's leading ladies)
Smoothly blended aged Jamaican and Haitian rums, spiced with rare herbs and balanced by lime juice and orange honey. A delicate glass of golden nectar.

HAWAIIAN COOLER **1.25**
(Originated beneath the cool swaying palms on Waikiki beach)
Delightfully chilled rums carefully poured over icy tropical juices. Exotic herbs heighten the flavor. A cooling adventure in drinking.

SOUTH PACIFIC PUNCH **1.00**
(Recalls the breezy atolls, and the soft breaking of the surf)
Aged Jamaica rum tempered with ripe lime juice. A mild drink typical of South Sea Island days.

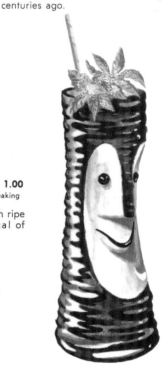

TIKI BOWL **2.00**
(The epitome of all Island drinks)
You will thrill to this innovation in drinking, as you sip delicate bouquets of rum from the unique Tiki Bowl. Thoughts of Island rituals come to mind as the rich aroma of this exotic drink is savored.

FOGG CUTTER **1.50**
(Uncrowned king of the exotic drinks)
Carefully measured portions of choice rum form the body as dashes of lemon juice, orgeat and orange honey combine to form a purely different flavor. Sipped slowly it has no equal among Polynesian drinks.

DIAMOND HEAD DAIQUIRI	1.00	GENERAL PATTON'S TANK	1.50
COBRA'S TOOTH	1.00	DR. FONG	1.50
PADRE'S PITFALL	1.00	SAMOAN TYPHOON (Limit of 2)	2.00
IMPATIENT VIRGIN	1.00	PAGO PAGO # 1	1.50
ZOMBIE	1.50	PAGO PAGO # 2	1.00
MAI TAI	1.50	PINA PEPE	1.75

Also your favorite American beverage

NAVY GROG **1.50**
(Limit of two to a customer)
A flotilla of Cuban, Puerto Rican and Demerara rums, mingle on a Bay of Pontchartrain sugar cane juice. Primed for action with the juice of a lime and the chill of ice. Will assure a sweetheart to every deck.

From riding the Zephyr to drinking my first Mai Tai, my most worthy formative experiences were at the beach, at the beach, at Pontchartrain Beach.

Walter Isaacson
Author

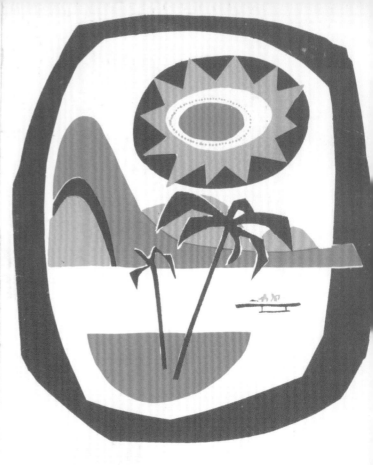

Bali Ha'i

at the bea

Rolling in the Deep

*I*n the fifties, the film *From Here to Eternity* was a smash hit, especially the sexy scene where Deborah Kerr and Burt Lancaster smooched in the sand among the crashing waves. According to the off-season Bali Ha'i night watchman, many similar encounters were discovered on the shores of Lake Pontchartrain. Apparently, several patrons would have one too many Mai Tais and attempt to reenact the amorous movie scene. The Beach definitely contributed to the baby boom.

Bryan

Harry Sr. entertaining Hollywood actresses Cleo Moore and France Nuyen. Cleo, originally from Baton Rouge, and France, best known for playing Liat in the blockbuster movie South Pacific, *signed autographs for fans during Beach appearances to promote their films.*

I remember Harry was such a wonderful man and dear friend. We would spend countless evenings at the Polynesian Paradise, good old Bali Ha'i.

Jimmy Fitzmorris
Former lieutenant governor, State of Louisiana

Gayle and John hosted debutante parties for their three nieces. Dancers groove to steel drums and guitars at Alyce Lee Jefferson's (far left) luau in the late sixties.

Oh, What a Night

I thought I was so special because my uncle Johnny owned the Beach! One of my favorite memories is the Hawaiian-themed debutante party that NanNan and Uncle Johnny gave for me and my sister, Debbie, at Bali Ha'i. As always, they pulled out all the stops. The Midway was lined with tiki torches and tropical flowers, and we danced under the moonlight. Best of all, everyone got "lei-d." It was the party of the season.

Paula Jefferson Jacobson

Floral sarongs and batik bermuda shorts were costume de rigueur. Alyce Lee (far right).

Jay, John, Gayle, and Bryan at the island soiree honoring Paula Jefferson Jacobson and Debbie Jefferson Schmitz in the early seventies.

Is Everybody Lit?

To dazzle us in the Bali Ha'i fun, Dad-ee had the mixologists create a concoction especially for his underage grandchildren. Tropical fruit juices with grenadine were poured over perfectly crushed ice, and the decorative garnish outshone any paper umbrella or dyed green maraschino cherry. The bartenders would hollow out a half of a lemon and add about one ounce of 151 rum, which was served ignited for a spectacular show. The Flaming Zorro was magical—found only in New Orleans, and only at the Bali Ha'i.

Bryan

Paula and Debbie with their uncle Johnny.

Some Enchanted Evening

When Peggy Scott Laborde, author and senior producer for New Orleans' PBS station, WYES-TV, and Errol Laborde, historian and editor in chief of *New Orleans Magazine* among many other publications, were planning their wedding reception, they knew it had to be at Pontchartrain Beach. One of their early dates included a starlit dinner at Bali Ha'i; Harry Batt, Sr., and Errol's father had been great friends; and Errol had fond memories of Flag Day as a Boy Scout, the day that hundreds of children had free access to all of the rides at the Beach. With its fabulous island decor, including an array of shells, glass buoys, and carved tiki sculptures, Bali Ha'i was the perfect romantic setting for a Big Easy wedding reception.

On May 28, 1977, the couple exchanged vows at St. Louis Cathedral before making their way up Elysian Fields to Bali Ha'i. It was one of the most festive places for special occasions in the city, and Peggy's description of the event is as charming as are the photographs. "I wore an organza hat, rather than a veil, which was different at the time. And Errol tossed Mardi Gras doubloons as we danced to the illustrious New Orleans Ragtime Orchestra. Our wedding cake was from Lombardi's on Carrollton Avenue and we served flaming volcanoes, pu pu platters, and Cantonese delicacies," she fondly described. "It just was a wonderful mix of our love for New Orleans and a truly one-of-a-kind place—the Beach."

Bali Ha'i Lite

Like many New Orleanians, I have always battled my weight. After years of having to shop in the husky section of department stores, I made up my mind when adolescence hit to shed the extra pounds. The Bali Ha'i was a godsend. I told the chefs that I wanted to trim down, and they were so supportive. Next thing I knew, when the deluxe Asian meals were delivered to our home (one of the best perks of the business ever), there were special dinners just for me: great low-calorie high-protein meals like deboned grilled chicken breast and steamed broccoli with shrimp. They didn't have to do it, but they did and it worked.

Jay

The Lemongrass Is Always Greener

When it came to cooking, Mom-ee was the star of the show. We still reminisce about her redfish courtbouillon, turkey hash, and Hungarian goulash. My mother, on the other hand, was not a culinary goddess, but she surely knew how to work a telephone and had Bali Ha'i on speed dial.

My first solid food was an eggroll, and I cut my teeth on Asian cuisine. That may seem exotic to some, but it was my peanut butter and jelly. Mom would call the restaurant and place our order, and the Sampan would make our special home delivery. While my friends' families ate red beans and rice on Mondays, we dined on sweet and sour chicken and shrimp fried rice. I got pretty tired of seeing those shiny covered trays come in the door bearing bamboo shoots and bok choy, so I did a little reconnaissance of my own. I discovered that my dad and the Bali Ha'i staff were eating good ole home cooking—smothered pot roast, fried chicken, and jambalaya. So as soon as I could dial a phone, I learned how to place my own standing dinner order: "I'll have whatever the staff is having. Thank you and no rush." Although my friends thought the Polynesian menu and amusement park were beyond exciting, I sometimes longed for a more typical life . . . a life where the father didn't work every day and night during the summer, the mother could bake a cake, and a pu-pu platter wasn't the equivalent of a grilled cheese.

Bryan

Testing, Testing, 1-2-3

My favorite childhood birthday party took place at the Beach when I turned eight. It was March 1, spring was in the air, and the Easter opening of the park was just around the corner. At this juncture in my youth, I was randomly into softball and Abbott and Costello movies, so my party-theme request was specific. Dad set up the 8mm projector in the main room of Bali Ha'i for a screening of black-and-white comedy clips, and we played a quick game of softball in an open field next to the restaurant. Later, as a surprise, he ushered my guests down the Midway to the east end of the park. I had not been in that area since the prior summer and was instantly ecstatic when I saw the new orange steel structure before me. Everyone was in awe. Then suddenly, my father, in his commanding voice, requested quiet as he announced that the boys of Newman class of 1981 would be the test riders of the very first steel rollercoaster in the South—the Galaxy! Needless to say, my eighth birthday definitely went down in the hall of fame and eclipsed all other Bali Ha'i birthday parties. Dad outdid himself.

Bryan

Father and son setting up the movie projector for Bryan's tenth-birthday party, 1973.

Cutting the cake at Bryan's eighth-birthday party, 1971. Left to right: Charles Stern, Gerald Williams, Bryan, and Dean Ecuyer.

BEST OF NEW ORLEANS .COM

gambit®

GAMBIT → VOLUME 31 → NUMBER 20 → MAY 18 → 2010

BALI HA'I Revisited

BY IAN MCNULTY

Pontchartrain Beach • NEW ORLEANS, LOUISIANA

SWIZZLE GUIDE TO WINE [PULLOUT]

Excuse Me While I Powder My Nose

There is one story that took place in the ladies' powder room at one dinner in the late 1950s that I will never forget. Several slightly inebriated girls entered wearing extremely full skirted prom dresses, as was the style. While they all giggled, preened, and primped, one precocious gal produced a Tiki Bowl. With the encouragement of her cohorts, she decided to swipe the bowl by placing it between her thighs, disguised beneath layer upon layer of crinoline petticoats. I followed her out and watched her painstakingly try to walk down the Midway without being caught. It was like watching an episode of "I Love Lucy." Although my initial response could have been to reprimand her, she had tried so hard and it was so comical . . . so, I figured, let her keep it; she earned it!

Fay Batt

Double daters enjoying signature dishes—pu-pu platters, eggrolls, and shrimp toast, 1970s. Left to right: Michael Farrell, Barbara, Cindy Abadie, Harry III.

Barbara and Martin D. Claiborne at their engagement party, 1976. Left to right: Fay, Barbara, Harry Jr., Marty.

My brothers would take their dates out for a sail and then come in to the pier, beeline to Bali Ha'i for drinks and food, and then sail back out in the moonlight. I never ratted them out.

Barbara

Gayle and John celebrating his thirtieth birthday and soon-to-be arrival of baby Jay.

Robert and Margaret Gerhardt's fortieth wedding anniversary, on June 12, 1981. Left to right: Sandra and Bobby Gerhardt, Robert and Margaret, Gilda and Billy Mares.

Harry Sr. and his lifelong friend, Eldred Drumm, celebrated many birthdays together. Here the Grand Poobahs say hello to sixty in 1963.

Entertaining industry friends from Australia. Left to right: John, Gayle, Geoffrey Thompson, Derrick Kidson, Fay, and Harry Jr.

Clockwise from far right: John, Gayle's sister Vilma Jefferson, Jack Denis, Dr. Sam St. Romain, and Fay.

Dining with best friends, early 1960s. Left to right: Bobby Zetzmann, Gayle, Harry Jr., Orite Zetzmann.

Left to right: Longtime general manager and promotional director George Rhode, sitting with John Batt, a guest, and Harry Batt, Jr.

The gang's all here for Marguerite's birthday, early 1960s. Left to right: Harry Jr., Harry III, David, Fay, Barbara, Harry Sr., Marguerite, Gayle, Jay, Bryan, John.

Friendly politics! Former New Orleans mayor Vic Schiro (back left) and his wife, Sunny (front left), entertaining Garr Moore and his wife, Mable.

Betty Woods minding the troops. Left to right: Ronald Randon, Harry III, David.

The Singhousers from Kentucky, Marguerite and Harry's dear friends from the amusement-park industry, celebrating their thirtieth wedding anniversary.

Marguerite (third from right) and her sisters.

Chapter 8
Beyond the Beach

Our greatest assets are our brain power, spirit, and desire.

Harry Batt, Sr., 1962

Keeping in mind that Harry Batt, Sr., left school at eighth grade, it is inspiring to see what one can do when tenacity and purpose align so closely with curiosity and independent thinking. Harry's entrepreneurial success and noted expertise in the amusement-park industry were marked by character traits not easily taught in even the best of business schools. With no act to follow locally and little competition anywhere in the South, Harry relied completely on self-direction and boundless optimism; obstacles were simply viewed as opportunities. His passion for the process of discovery, calculating risk, and acting on dreams made his life's vocation hardly seem like work. With powerful vision and energy, he contributed to the realization and economic growth of the lakefront area that we still enjoy today, and he never forgot his humble roots. Believing that society benefits when we all have access to education and the arts, he enriched the community with significant financial commitments to City Park, the New Orleans Museum of Art, Delgado College, and the New Orleans Recreation Department, which speaks volumes about his devotion to families and children beyond Pontchartrain Beach.

As an industry leader on an international scale, he was unrivaled in his enthusiasm for outdoor family entertainment. In 1949 and 1950, he served as president of the International Association of Amusement Parks and Attractions, a worldwide trade organization founded in 1918. He appeared before Congress over thirty times as chairman of the group's Legislative Committee to request tax relief for outdoor amusement parks, especially during wartime. He believed that parks and family recreation were assets to any community and as such should be afforded protection and support. His creed was: "Unlike champagne or perfume, parks are not luxuries; all children deserve recreation." In 1972, he received IAAPA's lifetime achievement award, and both Harry Jr. and John went on to serve on the organization's board for many years.

Harry and Marguerite were avid travelers for work and pleasure, which they considered one and the same. They routinely took months-long excursions around the globe, with extensive trips to South Africa, Europe, and Asia. Marguerite was a master packer and always kept her suitcases ready. Harry

Opposite: A flying horse at historic Carousel Gardens in City Park.

Jay and Gayle at the dedication of a City Park Carousel horse to John Batt, 1980s.

planned their itineraries with visits to the most modern hotels, suburbs, and architecture and the most famous outdoor treasures worldwide. Marguerite's meticulous travel journals and letters home illuminate their shared passion for adventure. In charming detail, she describes meeting park friends in every city for magnificent tours of places such as Tivoli Gardens in Denmark and Tiergarten in Austria and brand-new satellite cities and shopping malls in Copenhagen and Hamburg. She lists exciting aerial rides in the Swiss Alps, helicopter jaunts in Paris, and spectacular views of modern bridges, buildings, and sprawling cityscapes. They rose at six on most days, and their action-packed schedule included appointments with lighting designers and manufacturers of their favorite devices along with excursions to every renowned outdoor entertainment venue, fair, or festival.

We're in Munich enjoying the splendid Oktoberfest, where you have never seen more gaiety in your life. It's like Pontchartrain Beach on Fourth of July. Besides all the concessions and rides, there are seven Beer Parlors with bands and dancing. Harry tried a few of the new devices, one of which we have seen before but never dared to try—the Toboggan where you fly down a chute on a mat. We all watched wondering if he would make it or fall flat on his fanny. Well, folks, he made it like a trooper.

Marguerite Batt, 1961

Reading the entries that displayed her great sense of humor and up-for-anything attitude brought her personality to life. She writes about shopping for music boxes, marzipan, and hand-knit sweaters for the grandchildren, while Harry considered the latest camera "that he is not sure that he should spend so much money on." She describes the yodeling tavern they stumbled on ("when in Rome") and the roadside pub where "Harry acted like he'd never seen bratwurst before." But her lively accounts of the evening activities made one thing clear; these two loved the nightlife. They joined friends and colleagues at swanky nightclubs for champagne and fine dining, attended revues and variety shows of every kind, and heard the best operas and concerts in every city. But the thing they loved most was dancing. There are notes about dancing well into the wee hours night after night, with fun jottings about the music, cocktails, and great hospitality they enjoyed everywhere they traveled.

With firsthand insight into this dynamic couple's approach to life comes a deep understanding of their motivations and priorities, which are nothing short of inspirational. Harry Sr.'s codirection of the Gayway at the Seattle

Humpty Dumpty and Little Bo Peep grace the new entrance.

World's Fair in 1962 was the perfect bookend to his fateful trip to the Chicago World's Fair in 1933, and it placed his talent on a world stage far beyond Pontchartrain Beach. For New Orleanians, the Beach represents a bygone era of prosperous camaraderie that lives on in our collective memories, and for that we are grateful. But for everyone who reads this story, we hope that the spirit of Harry and Marguerite's ingenuity and pluck goes far beyond the confines of any one place and time, as we consider new obstacles as splendid opportunities.

Flying Horses

The longest-standing amusement attraction in New Orleans is at City Park and has a deep history with the Batt family. The magnificent wooden Carousel, which has existed since 1906, was operated and lovingly maintained by the Batts for many decades when Pontchartrain Beach was open. Albeit not the most lucrative of ventures, Playland Amusements, the parent company of the Beach, was the ideal steward for the continuous restoration and care of this rare piece of American art.

Many of the animals date back to the late 1800s and were carved and hand painted by the master carver Charles Looff, who also designed and built the first merry-go-round at Coney Island. His Flying Horses, named for the steeds that go up and down as the Carousel turns, are known for their flamboyant, highly decorated style, bedazzled with faux gems and real horse hair. The fifty-three gorgeous stallions are examples of the stylistic influence he would have on many other renowned carvers.

The Carousel, one of only 100 wooden carousels still intact in the country, has a lion, camel, giraffe, and two chariots in addition to the horses. It is powered by its original 1906 motor, and its 1915 Wurlitzer band organ continues to entertain us with circus music. The Carousel is on the National Register of Historic Places and will forever hold a cherished place in the city's heart.

The few kiddie rides that Playland Amusements operated in City Park never had the kind of attendance that Pontchartrain Beach did, making it a costly enterprise to maintain. In 1956, inspired by the garden of vibrant, over-the-top fairytale characters he saw at Children's Fairyland in Oakland, California, Harry decided to create something similar here in hopes of attracting more families to the park. He commissioned New Orleanian artist Josef Lentz to design thirteen oversized, perspective-skewed attractions, such as Peter Pan and Mother Goose, that tykes could climb and play on while indulging their imaginations. Storyland opened in December of that year to enormous success, with 500,000 people visiting the park in the first year. Since then, thirteen sculptures have been commissioned by City Park and built by Blaine Kern Artists over the years. This children's fantasy playland still sits under the grand century-old oak trees today, welcoming the child in all of us.

The original Pinocchio and Blue Whale.

Above: The Little Old Lady Who Lived in a Shoe.

Children at play on the City Park railroad, 1960s.

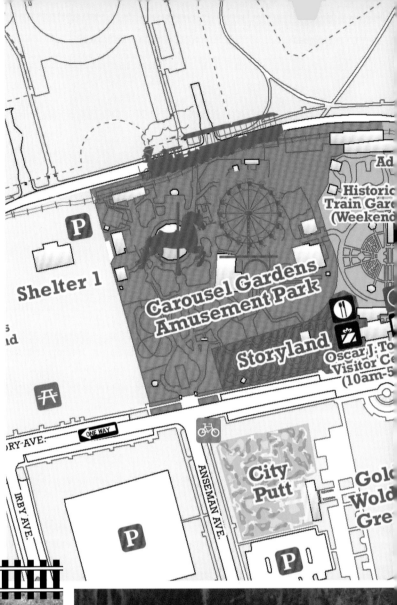

Shelter 1

Carousel Gardens Amusement Park

Storyland

City Putt

Ad

Historic Train Gare (Weekend

Oscar J. To Visitor Ce (10am-5

Gol Wol Gre

ONE WAY

The recently refurbished City Park miniature train is a delight for children of all ages. The ride is especially beautiful during the park's Celebration in the Oaks, which is held yearly during the holiday season.

An evening ride under the oaks.

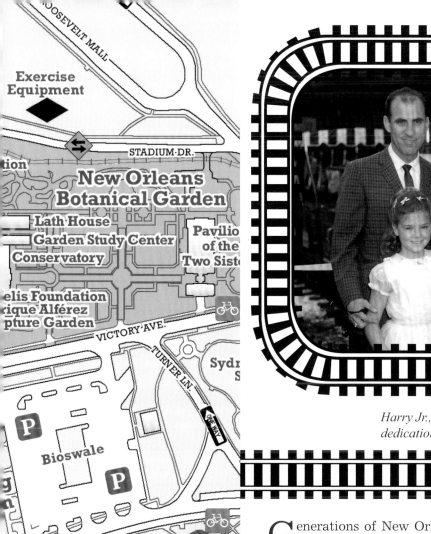

Harry Jr., Barbara, Gayle, Jay, and John at the
dedication of the City Park railroad in 1962.

Generations of New Orleans youth have enjoyed a miniature train ride throughout City Park since 1898. The enchanting two-mile ride around the stunning gardens and under the massive oak trees dripping with Spanish moss is one of the most popular attractions in the city. For many decades, Playland Amusements maintained and operated the train, ensuring it received the tender loving care it required. In the early sixties, the train was refurbished and in 1962 the brightly colored ride was dedicated to the park with great fanfare. Today, tykes can still take the same ride that delighted their great-grandparents over one hundred years ago, and that is a tradition we all hold dear.

In 1963, Harry Batt, Sr., directed the installation of the miniature railroad line at the St. Louis Zoo and operated it for several years with great success. Modeled after the original C. P. Huntington, a famous steam locomotive first built in 1863, this scaled-back replica is the largest in the country. Originally named the Zooline Railroad, it is now the Emerson Zooline Railroad, in gratitude for a five million dollar gift from Emerson Electric to be used to maintain this beautiful American treasure.

To Catch a Thief

My brother, Jay, always seemed to be embroiled in some sort of high-stakes adventure. One summer while he was working the railroad in City Park, there was a robbery occurring in a bordering neighborhood. When Jay noticed policemen running his way, he jumped into action and signaled for them to climb onboard. The chase ensued full steam ahead. At the other end of the tracks, fellow officers were closing in on the culprit, and shortly he was caught. As it turns out, one of those "trainspotting" cops was New Orleans' future chief of police, Eddie Compass.

Bryan

Harry Batt and the Seattle World's Fair

The Seattle World's Fair in 1962, dubbed the Century 21 Exposition, was one of the most influential and exciting international fairs ever. Major fairs had been held regularly in the United States from the 1850s through 1940, but World War II broke that continuity. When the Seattle Fair was conceived, there had not been a fair in over twenty years, and in those years, there had been seismic waves of change in almost every cultural arena. With the Space Race and Cold War well under way, Americans were eager to display their dominance in aerospace, science, technology, and all things futuristic. The eyes of the world were on Seattle.

In 1959, Harry Batt and his colleague, Patty Conklin of Canada, were two of North America's leading amusement-park owners at the pinnacle of their careers. With a third partner, Jack Ray, the most modern amusement-facade designer in the world, they decided to pitch to the Seattle planners the right to assemble an expansive midway at the fair, befitting the nation's optimism. They were experts in the industry with sterling reputations, so their stunning proposal, filled with avant-garde drawings and dynamic vision, landed a staggering two million dollar contract and complete control of the fair's midway. Such free rein of a midway had never been given before, and the outdoor-amusement industry was astonished.

Their dazzling, space-themed Gayway was the first profitable midway ever at a world's fair, and the co-directors still hold that record today. This crowning achievement of a New Orleanian inspired by the Chicago World's Fair of 1938 was nothing short of spectacular and is a testament to Harry's forward-thinking and vast imagination. The early sixties were heady times marked by youth-driven enthusiasm for change—the perfect fuel for Harry's extraordinary creative energy. Twenty glittering rides with colorful facades and splendid loading stations lined the Gayway, and the renowned Velare Brothers built many of the devices including the Seattle Sky Wheel, the world's largest Ferris wheel at the time. The Trip to Mars, Space Whirl, Italian Meteor, and German Wild Maus captured the world's best in technological innovation. The Gayway exploded with American confidence.

Ten million people attended the six-month-long exposition, including presidents, celebrities, and royalty; but at thirty-five cents a ride, the midway appealed to the working man and his family, which had always been the key to Harry's success. For the first time, television advertisements and national periodicals played a major role in spotlighting the fair, and throngs of patrons poured into the amusement zone. At ninety-eight feet high, the Sky Wheel was second in popularity only to the Space Needle. After the fair closed, the city continued the wildly successful Gayway as the Fun Forest until 2011, and now the Chihuly Garden and Glass sits on this storied site.

And as fate would have it, Elvis Presley and Harry Batt's paths crossed again in Seattle. The movie *It Happened at the World's Fair* was filmed on the Gayway, and scene after scene was shot of Elvis and his costar Vicky Tiu on the Sky Wheel. When the feature premiered in 1963, once again all eyes were on Seattle.

We toured the plant in Waldkirch, Germany that is making four devices for us for the Seattle World's Fair. We saw the welding, woodwork, and some of the finished art figures that will lend so much interest to the rides.

Marguerite Batt, 1961

The senior Batts held a lavish Seattle-themed party on New Year's Eve 1962 at their home at the Beach to celebrate Marguerite's birthday and the success of the World's Fair. Clockwise from top right: Harry Sr., Gayle expecting Bryan, John, Fay, Marguerite, and Harry Jr.

In 1955, Harry Sr. reigned as king of the Mystic Krewe of Hermes, the longest continuously night parading Mardi Gras krewe in New Orleans, founded in 1937. Dawn Hébert—daughter of former U.S. representative F. Edward Hébert, who named the organization—was his queen.

Harry Sr. toasts his queen at Gallier Hall.

Fay (fourth from left), Marguerite (center), and John's fiancée, Gayle (second from right), viewing the pageantry of the ball held at the Municipal Auditorium.

It's Good to Be the King

In 1972, Barbara and my grandfather reigned as king and queen of the Louisiana Mardi Gras Ball in Washington, D.C. Jay and I served as royal pages to their majesties. Dad-ee donned his Hermes duds again for this regal occasion. Years later, I discovered the bejeweled costume in storage and have loved sporting his tunic on Mardi Gras Day every year since.

Bryan

Barbara and her grandfather photographed at the New Orleans Museum of Art.

For years Endymion planned to build a super float, and we searched to find just the right iconic image to represent New Orleans. After much thought, my idea was to honor the Batt family for the many years of fun and entertainment they gave to the people of our community. So we designed the largest float in the history of Mardi Gras, with nine sections connected together, carrying 270 riders, and we called it "Pontchartrain Beach: Then and Now."

Edmond "Ed" Muniz
Founder and captain of the Krewe of Endymion

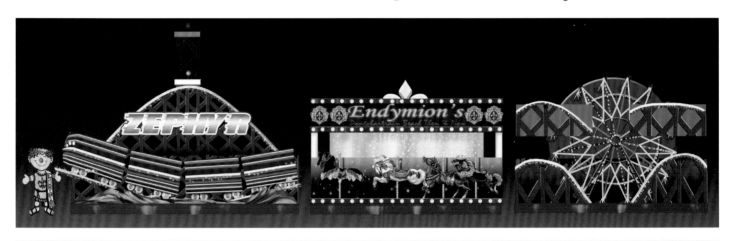

Artwork and photographs of the largest Mardi Gras float in history, Pontchartrain Beach, in the Endymion parade.

The Midway on Wheels

During the 2013 Carnival season, the Mardi Gras superkrewe Endymion unveiled the largest and longest float ever produced in the world—a reincarnation of the storied landmark, Pontchartrain Beach. Parade-goers were simply speechless at the sight of this magnificent 375-foot extravaganza that recreated the beloved amusement park in such glorious detail. During the design phase of this massive undertaking, the Batt family shared old photographs and memories with Barry Kern of Kern Studios and his brilliant team of artists and Ed Muniz, the Endymion krewe captain. The finished work, an opulent spectacle recreating the Midway in all its glory, far surpassed their wildest imaginations. The float is made up of nine linked sections that fully depict iconic attractions from the park's heyday in masterworks of sculpture, paint, lighting, and sound. The pioneering spirit and vision of Kern Studios and the Endymion krewe truly capture the spirit of Pontchartrain Beach. When the parade rolls annually on the Saturday evening before Mardi Gras, it is easily one of the most spectacular happenings in the city all year. Two hundred and seventy maskers, loaded with thousands and thousands of pounds of doubloons and throws, many of them Pontchartrain Beach themed, ride on the multilevel float complete with the Zephyr, Haunted House, Wild Maus, and clown head as it snakes through the streets of New Orleans. The Musik Express blasts the top forty of the era, the Carousel is lighted with stunning computer-run technology, and the scents of burgers, fried onions, and cotton candy are pumped into the air, creating an over-the-top entertainment experience. We know that Harry Sr., John, and Harry Jr. would be delighted by such a stellar display of talent. Just as the Beach did for decades, Kern Studios and Endymion excite and inspire New Orleanians year after year.

When You Wish Upon a Star

*I*n 2002, Mom proclaimed that my nieces Bailey and Kelly were of the "proper age" for their maiden voyage to Disney World, and she began to plan and over-plan a grand family trip. I think—rather, I know—that Mom was equally as or maybe even more excited than the girls. She reminisced about our long-lasting Disney friendship and wanted her grandchildren to experience the same magical connection. She enlisted Tom to write an eloquent and sentimental letter to the president of Disney World, claiming that he was such a better writer than she. Gayle Batt always knew how to get things done, and she often cajoled Tom into assisting her. Tom wrote a beautiful letter describing my mom's fond memories of her honeymoon at Disneyland, my grandfather's professional relationship with Walt Disney, and our upcoming family vacation. Upon arrival, we were thrilled to learn that our accommodations had been upgraded to the most gorgeous Grand Floridian suites with stunning views of Cinderella's castle; our princesses were in awe. We were treated to fast passes, champagne, and fresh fruit daily, and meals were with costumed characters—I think we actually had a snack with Mufasa! Never in our wildest dreams could we imagine such gracious hospitality, but apparently the roots of the amusement-park world run deep. The trip was everything that my mom had hoped it would be; therefore, she entrusted Tom with writing the thank-you note that she sent along with king cakes (but of course).

Bryan

Andree and Jay's daughters, Kelly (left) and Bailey, with Mickey Mouse, the top chef, 2002.

Clockwise from top left: Bryan, a ghoul from the Haunted House, Tom, Jay, and Andree, Halloween 2015.

To the Battmobile

Several years ago, while rushing to an appointment, I thought I caught a glimpse of a familiar ghoulish face. I pulled my car over to investigate, and although it was almost completely hidden in the garage of a home, sure enough I did know that scary mug. It was the skeleton car from the Haunted House. Because I was in a hurry, I wrote down the address rather than ringing the bell. The next day, I mentioned it to Andree, and the scheme was born. We would procure the car and have it restored, and it would be the perfect Christmas gift from Andree to Jay. She wrote to the residents, and as fate would have it, they remembered us boys. Everything worked out perfectly, Jay was overwhelmed with the unexpected memorabilia, and now it proudly sits in front of their home every year as the perfect decoration for the neighborhood Halloween party. I love a good "Scooby-Doo" ending!

Bryan

Souvenirs and memorabilia represent the heart and soul of our beloved shared experience. Clockwise from top left: An IAAPA convention glass, ashtray 1970s, painted tin sign 1920s, decorative tray 1960s, pennant 1970s, bolts from the Zephyr after demolition 1983, a rare Elvis Presley fan 1956, P.O.P. ticket stub that survived Hurricane Katrina, Frisbee 1970s, matchbook 1960s, pennant 1970s, restaurant paper placemat early 1950s, P.O.P. bracelet 1970s, a pageant trophy that survived Hurricane Katrina 1930s.

If I had one more hour at Pontchartrain Beach, I would . . .

. . . ride the Zephyr and the bumper cars and walk the Midway while "Summer in the City" was playing. Before the hour was up, I'd walk out on the beach and gaze at the sunset.

Donna Richert

. . . sit on the sand and watch the boat-stage entertainment or the trapeze artists and walk the Midway, people watching and smelling the wonderful mixture of salty lake water and greasy burgers. The only sounds I hear are people laughing and screaming, having the time of their lives.

Priscilla Cousans Schroeder

. . . ride the planes and have a Fogg Cutter at the Bali Ha'i while listening to "A Summer Place" and dreaming about Troy Donahue.

Cheryl B. Ermon

. . . come in the Zephyr entrance and ride it twice, then off to the Log Flume and old-time arcade, with the gunman who drew against you and other classic games. Then I'd hotfoot it to the YoYo and Musik Express. Dang—out of time!

Kenneth Flenner

. . . want to just stroll along and people watch, maybe take the Sky Ride to get a bird's-eye view of everything. I wouldn't pick a song; the sounds of the park and New Orleanians having fun would be mind-blowing as it is.

Tim San Fillippo

. . . walk the Midway, loving the sounds and the smell. I'd meet up with my friends from an early sixties WTIX Night. The pool, the beach house, the key to a locker pinned to my bathing suit are all wonderful memories of family fun.

Necha Otillio Murphy

. . . enjoy one last walk down the Midway, ride the Wild Maus, visit Kiddieland, ride the Ferris Wheel, and walk barefoot in the sand while eating cotton candy and singing "Good Day Sunshine."

Norma Jean Bostic

. . . ride the Flying Scooters and the Bug, and hopefully Adventures in Space is back open. Then I'd hit the arcade, shooting gallery, and Sky Ride for one last look at everything. "Mr. Big Stuff" by Jean Knight plays the whole time.

Lawrence P. Beron

. . . ride the Zephyr and the Galaxy and try to squeeze in the Musik Express or the Bug. I would walk up and down the Midway just taking it all in. Next, I would go to the penny arcade to make a metal keychain from the machine that made the round good-luck charms, and of course go to the fortuneteller lady. Then I would have to hop on the Sky Ride before heading back towards the Zephyr to ride again. Last thing I would do would be to take tons of pictures, which I wish I would have done years ago.

Connie T. Randazzo

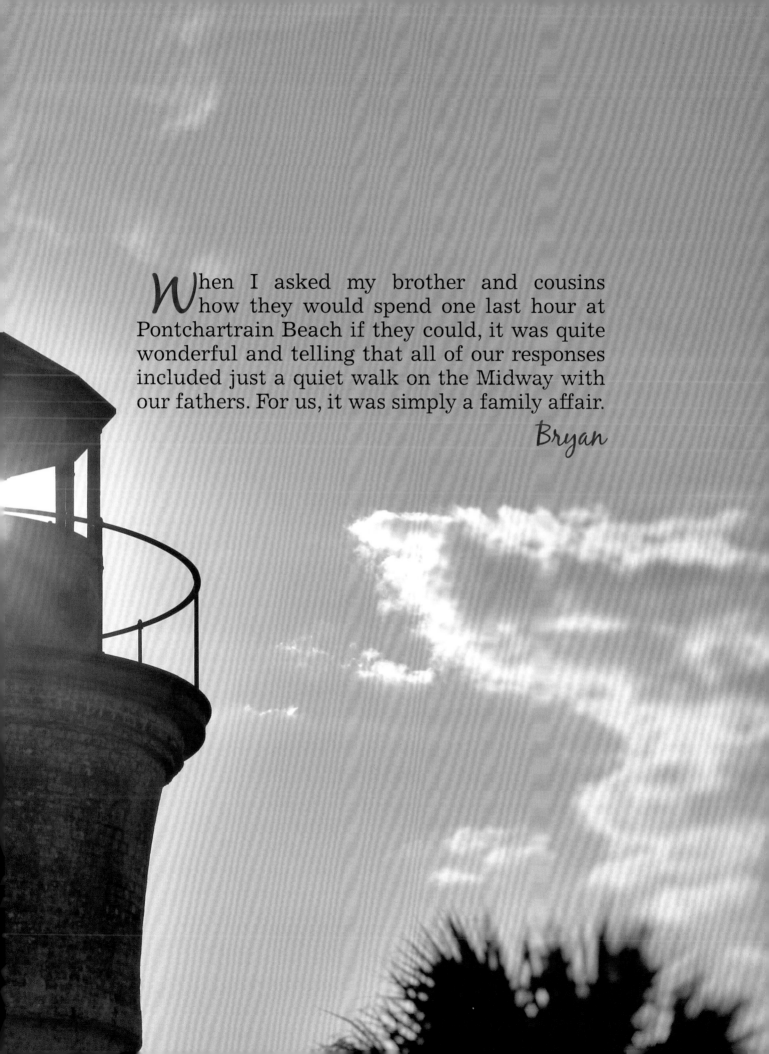

When I asked my brother and cousins how they would spend one last hour at Pontchartrain Beach if they could, it was quite wonderful and telling that all of our responses included just a quiet walk on the Midway with our fathers. For us, it was simply a family affair.

Bryan

Credits

NOLA.com | The Times-Picayune and The States-Item supported *Pontchartrain Beach* from the very beginning. Without this mutually positive relationship, the story of the Beach would be difficult to tell. We are sincerely grateful to The Times-Picayune for providing us photographs for inclusion in our book. The following page numbers reflect their generosity:

24, 48, 50, 57, 62, 68, 72, 75, 94 top, 97, 98, 101 center, 120 center, 132, 136, 137, 138 top, 150, 153, 168 top left, 172 top, 179 bottom, 213 (© The Times-Picayune Publishing Co. All rights reserved. Used with permission of The Times-Picayune.)

The Pontchartrain Beach community stretches near and far and we treasure each and every story we received. We could have easily tripled the number of pages in the book with all of the mementos and pictures that were so kindly shared with us in an outpouring of support for our project. The following photographs are courtesy of:

Evangeline Albaral, 80 top right
Karen Anglada, 117 bottom left
Henry Beck, 77 top
Catherine Campanella, 16
Colleen Dempsey Carmichael, 131
Stephanie Carra, 118 bottom left
Francis Celino, 219
City Park New Orleans, 204, 206, 207, 208 bottom left
Erin Collins, 119 top
Douglas Degan, 25, 32 top, 103 bottom
Pam Georges Dongieux, 119 bottom
Marlin Bourg Donham, 179 bottom left
Leslie Smith Everage, 106 top right
Figaro, 148
Edwin Fleischmann, 109 bottom
Genie Kennon Fleishel, 106 top left and bottom left
Gambit, 198
Joan Boudousquie Garvey, 117 top
The Historic New Orleans Collection, 18, 88 bottom, 144, 172 bottom, 182 bottom, 183 bottom left
Vanessa Hammler Kenon, 108, 109 top
Kern Studios, 214, 215 top and bottom
Tracey Knoepfler, 218
Peggy Scott Laborde, 194, 195
Chip Landry, 81 bottom, 84 bottom
Kevin Mackenroth, 215 center
Gilda Mares, 80 bottom right, 200 center

Ruben Mazariegos, 138 bottom, 171
Frank Minyard, 170
Necha Otillio Murphy, 168 bottom right
New Orleans Magazine, 54, 56 top, 65, 101 border, 120 border
Mike Perry, 152
David Pons, 64 bottom
Greg Randall, 179 top
Deborah Jefferson Schmitz, 80 top left and center right
Barney M. Seely, 118 top right
Jane Sikes, 66 bottom left
Gerald Stagg, 76 bottom
David Tarantino, 14, 17, 58, 66 top, 69
Craig Trentecosta, 20, 28, 30, 111, 158, 161, 162, 163
Kathleen Langla Truxillo, 176, 177
Cherie Vitrano, 149
Bob Walker, 80 bottom left
Cassandra Watson, 32 bottom, 66 bottom right, 117 bottom right, 156
Arthur Wehl, 188 top left
Lisa Gerhardt Williams, 76 top, 135
Chris Young, 60, 102

Photography credits:
G. E. Arnold, 101 center, 120 center
Charles F. Bennett, 57, 94 top
Lawrence Beron, 70
Kurt Coste, 104
Joe DeMajo, 61, 85 top, 93 bottom, 116, 124, 128
Steven Forster, 217
James Gaffney, 53
Philip Gaurisco, 75 top
Chip Landry, 1, 49, 90, 91, 92, 218, 219
Anne King Levert, 64 bottom
Jerry Lodrigues, 137 top
George Long, 5
Mike Posey, 52
Denis Poupart, 74, 89, 146, 147, 166, 168 bottom left, 171, 188 bottom left, 208 bottom right
Connie Randazza, 219
Doug Sanders, 220
Burt Steel, 137 bottom
Tipery Studios, 194, 195
Jim Whitmore, 54, 56 top, 65, 101 border, 120 border

All other photos and materials courtesy of the Batt family collection.

Acknowledgments

We've dreamed about writing this book for almost a decade, reminiscing and brainstorming about how we would go about capturing the essence and magic of such an iconic institution. It felt pretty daunting. But we knew if we trained our eye on the why, how, and what that could make such a phenomenon happen, we could bring our unique voice and fresh perspectives to a story that so many people feel they already know so well.

We both love the art of communication and believe that entertainment in any form speaks to our shared humanity. By studying Pontchartrain Beach from the many interrelated facets of American culture—fashion, music, food trends, movies, and the social mores of the era—we can see that the park's popularity was the result of so much more than the rides and attractions. People sharing a collective experience in a certain time and place—that's the story we wanted to tell.

So many people near and far opened their hearts to us as they shared memories and photographs. Through faded pictures and family lore, the personality of the Beach was back on center stage with such great emotion. We received a wealth of information from the community, from poignant personal stories to universal ones, and we are deeply grateful. This is by no means intended to be an exhaustive documentation of all things Beach. We know that the accuracy of stories fades in the retelling, but we also know that the overall message is authentic. Thanks to each of you who helped us understand what the Beach meant to you.

Thank you to Jay, Harry Jr., Barbara, and David for spending hours with us laughing and answering questions as we put together pieces of the family puzzle. Our story is your story.

The following people kindly provided valuable information as we researched for the book: Ruben Mazariegos, Craig Trentacosta, Denis Poupart, Joe DeMajo, Chip Landry, David Tarantino, and Greg Salling.

Thank you to the *New Orleans Times-Picayune, Gambit, Figaro, New Orleans Magazine, New Orleans Advocate,* The Historic New Orleans Collection, and City Park for sharing your archives with us so that photographs and content from local publications could be included in the book.

Pelican Publishing Company embraced our project from the very beginning. Thank you to the entire team at Pelican, especially our editor, Nina Kooij, for your excitement and expertise. It goes without saying that having our book published in New Orleans brings us immense pride.

As always, we are thankful for our entire Hazelnut staff. Our talented colleagues are willing to wear so many creative hats in support of our projects and this camaraderie is what makes our company so special and unique.

We spent the summer of 2017 devoted to writing this book after two years of research. Meredith Peltier, our editorial assistant, worked daily to fact check and document our stacks of letters and photographs. Her organizational skills and love of musical theatre made for some really fun moments on some very long days. The Pontchartrain Beach Facebook group, with over twelve thousand members, inspired us daily with endless leads and unbridled enthusiasm. And lastly, we are grateful for the women at our neighborhood Langenstein's, who cheered us on when we stopped by twice daily for snacks, lunch, and friendly faces. We can't wait to bring you books!

Index

Pontchartrain Beach Amusement Park on Lake Shore Drive,
New Orleans, La.

PONCHARTRAIN BEACH AND AMUSEMENT PARK, NEW ORLEANS, LA.

PONTCHARTRAIN BEACH
AMUSEMENT PARK,
NEW ORLEANS, LA. — 47

Pontchartrain Beach
New Orleans, La.

Pontchartrain Beach
New Orleans, La.

DISNEY
PIRATES of the CARIBBEAN
ON STRANGER TIDES

ISBN 978-1-4584-1185-3

Disney characters and artwork © Disney Enterprises, Inc.

WALT DISNEY MUSIC COMPANY

DISTRIBUTED BY

HAL•LEONARD®
CORPORATION

7777 W. BLUEMOUND RD. P.O. BOX 13819 MILWAUKEE, WI 53213

In Australia Contact:
Hal Leonard Australia Pty. Ltd.
4 Lentara Court
Cheltenham, Victoria, 3192 Australia
Email: ausadmin@halleonard.com.au

Visit Hal Leonard Online at
www.halleonard.com

GUILTY OF BEING INNOCENT OF BEING JACK SPARROW

Music by HANS ZIMMER

Moderately fast, in 2

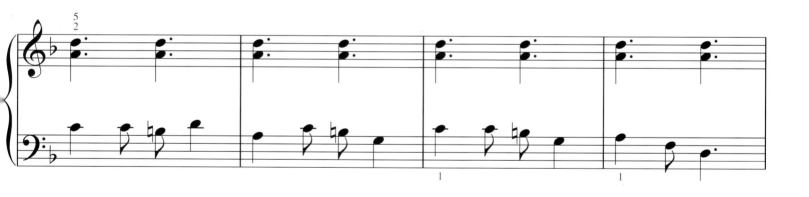

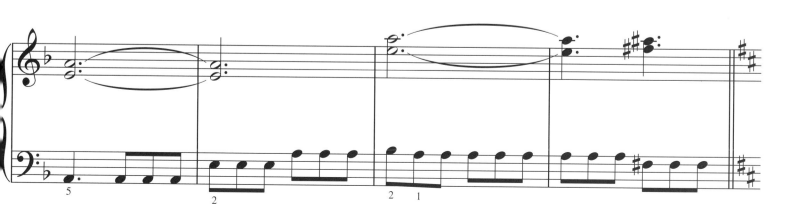

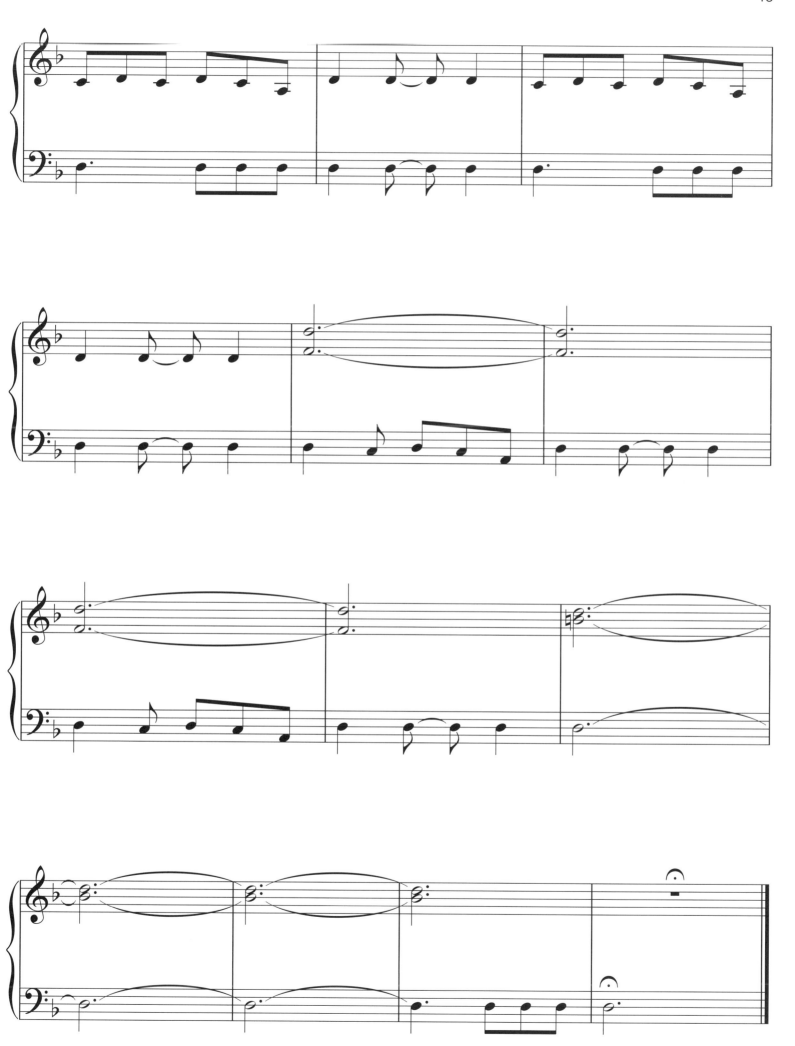

ANGELICA

Music by HANS ZIMMER,
EDUARDO CRUZ, RODRIGO SANCHEZ
and GABRIELA QUINTERO

Moderate Bolero

To Coda ⊕

D.S. al Coda

CODA

MUTINY

Music by HANS ZIMMER

Fast, driving

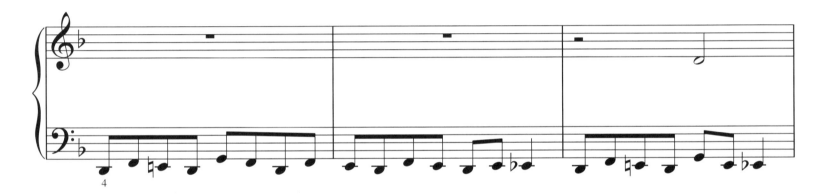

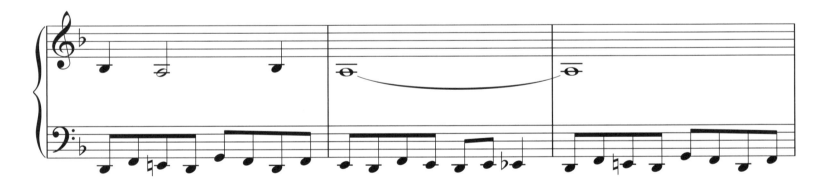

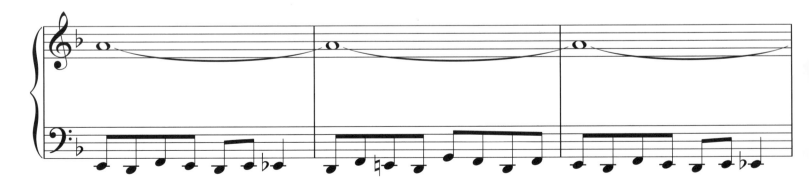

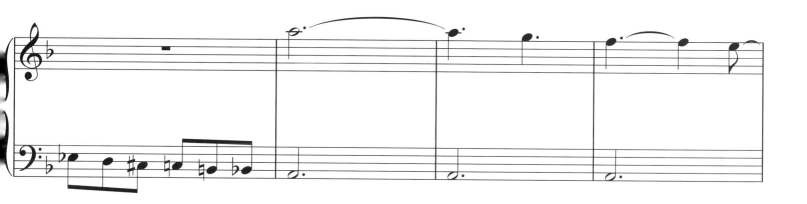

Moderately fast

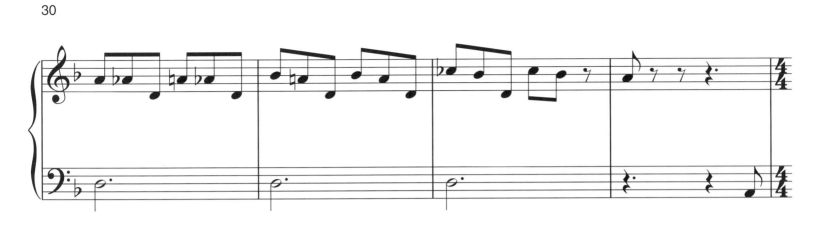

Play 7 times

THE PIRATE THAT SHOULD NOT BE

Music by RODRIGO SANCHEZ,
GABRIELA QUINTERO and HANS ZIMMER

Moderately fast

Faster

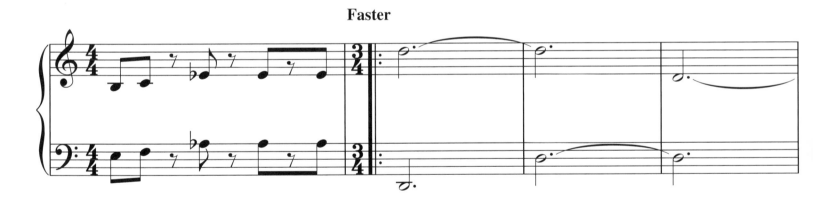

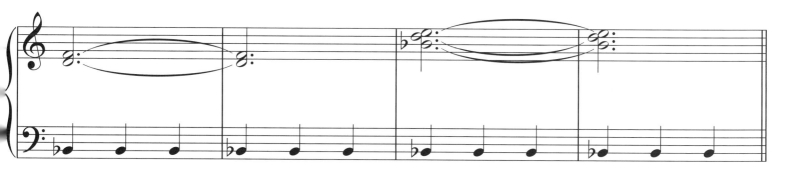

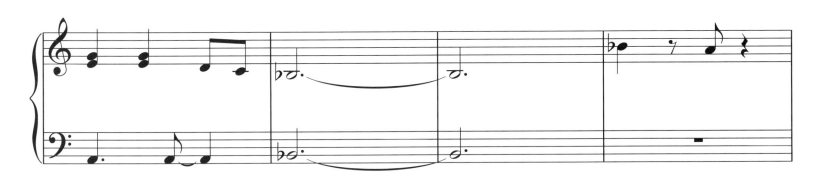

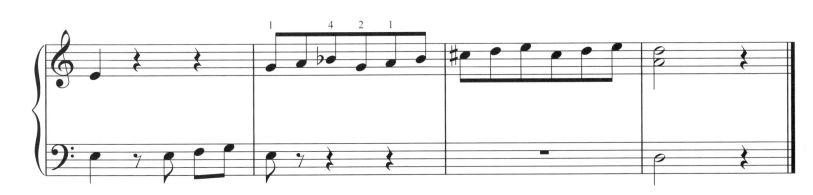

MERMAIDS

Music by HANS ZIMMER
and ERIC WHITACRE

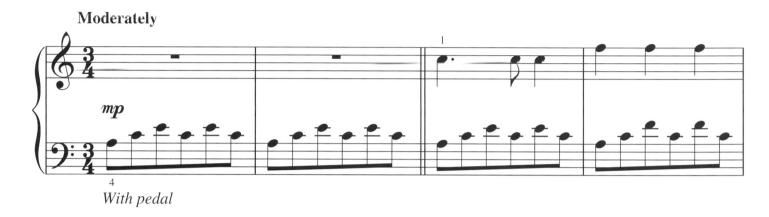

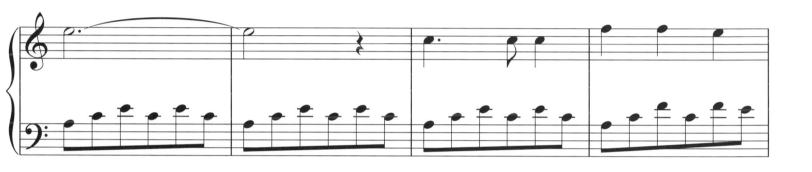

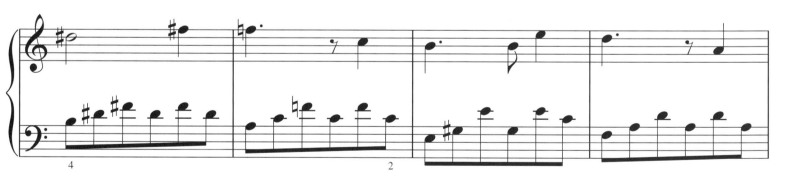

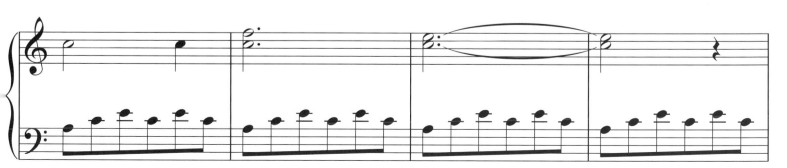

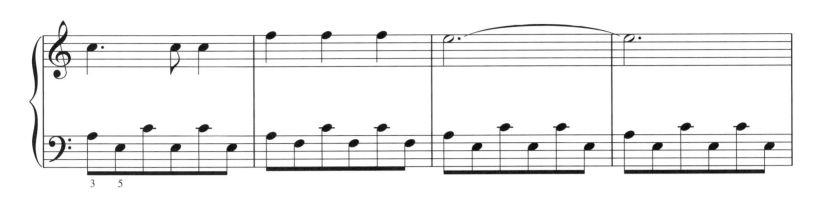

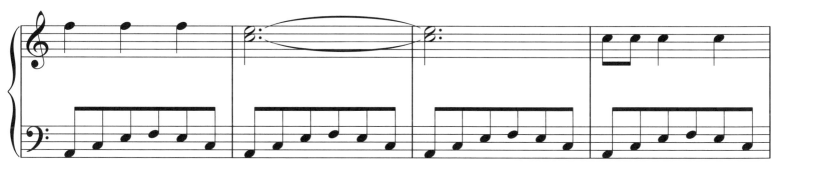

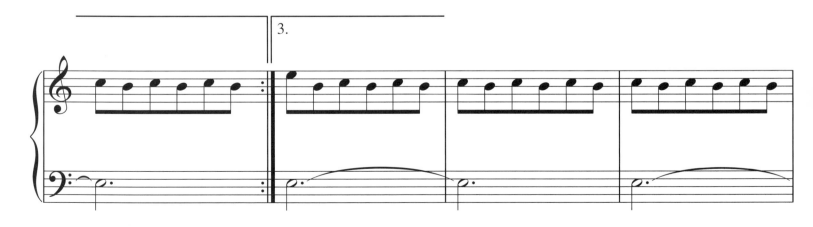

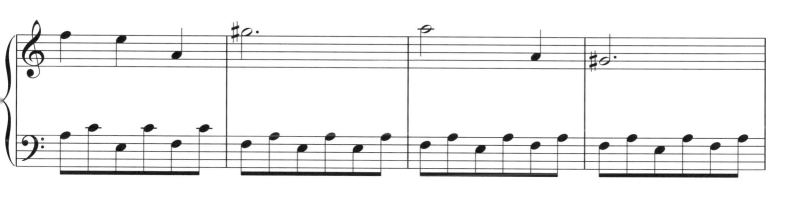

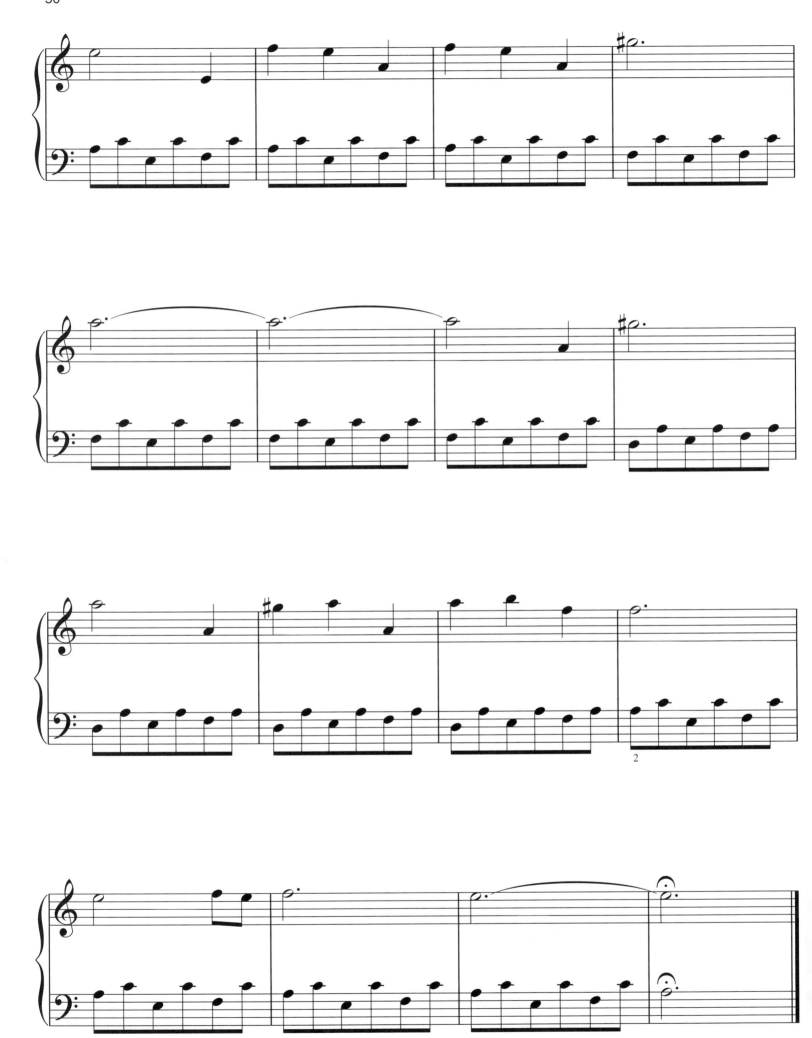

SOUTH OF HEAVEN'S CHANTING MERMAIDS

Music by RODRIGO SANCHEZ,
GABRIELA QUINTERO and HANS ZIMMER

Moderately

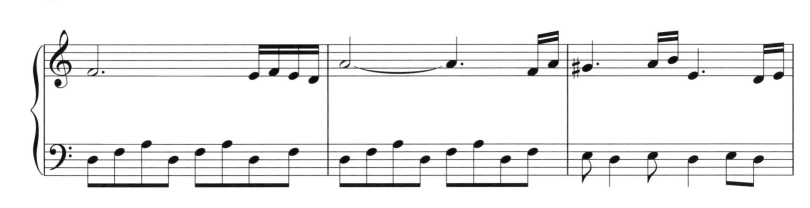

To Coda ⊕

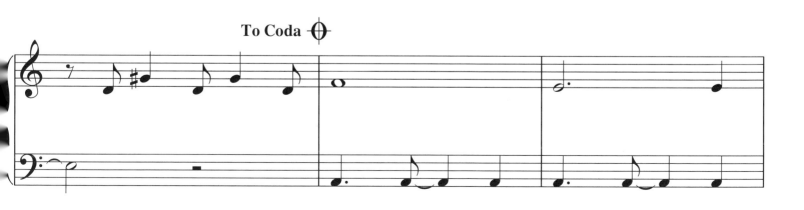

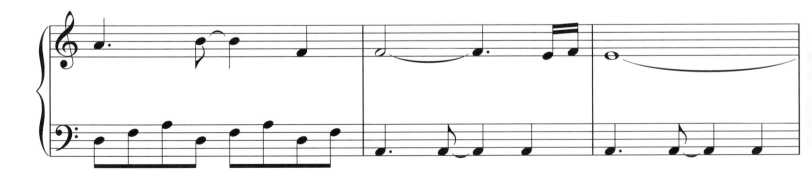

D.S. al Coda

CODA

Play 3 times

PALM TREE ESCAPE

Music by HANS ZIMMER

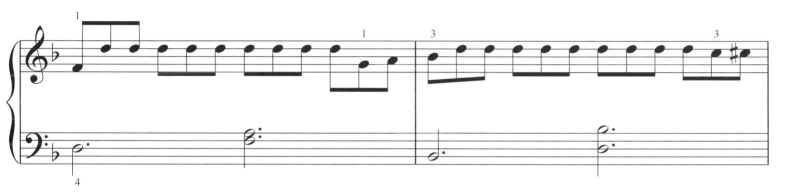

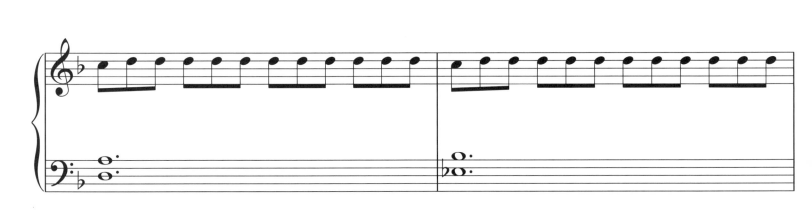

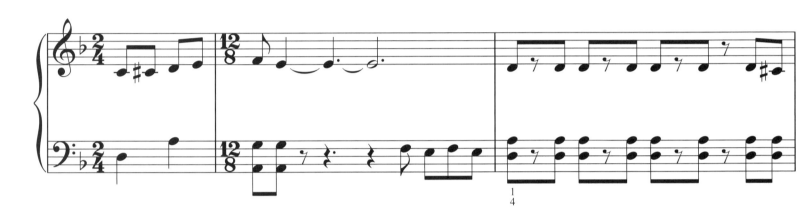

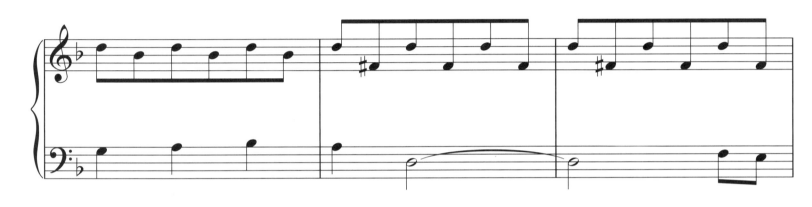

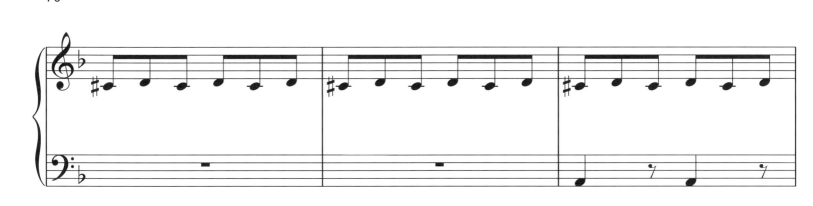

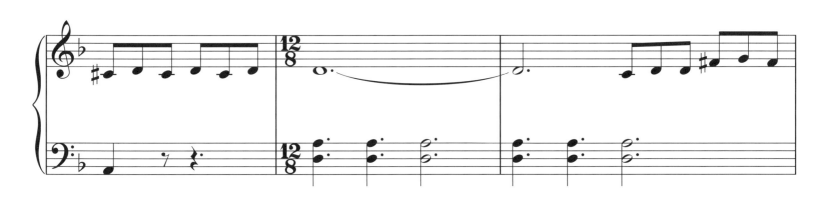

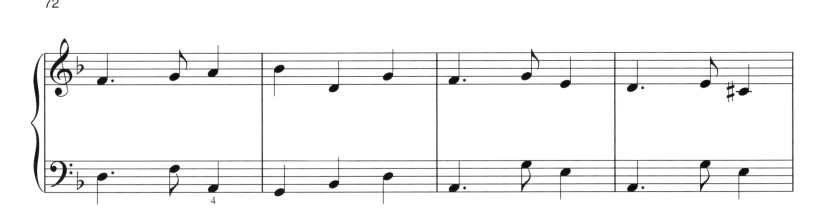

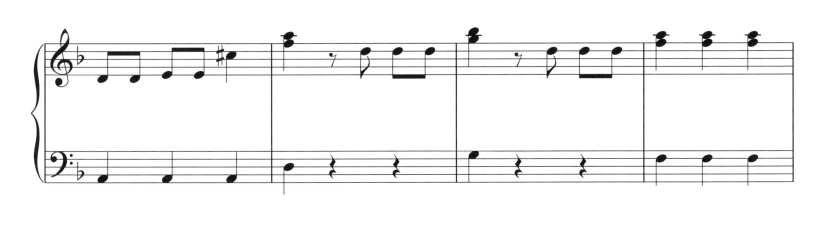

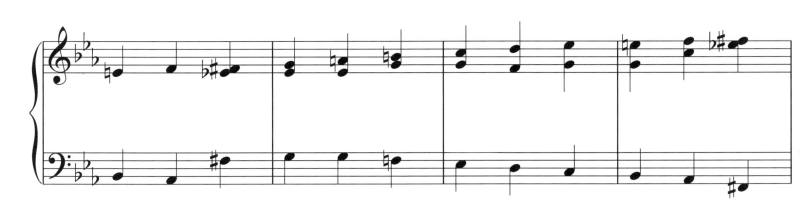

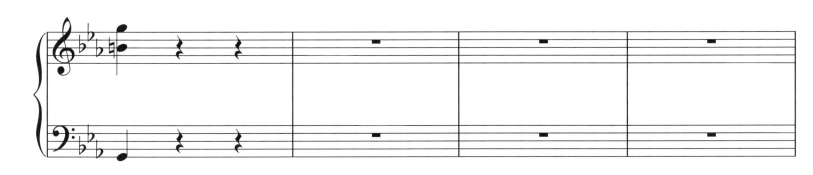

BLACKBEARD

Music by HANS ZIMMER

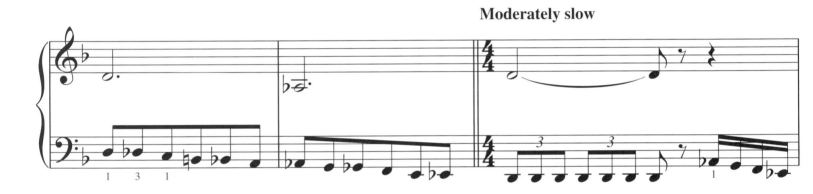

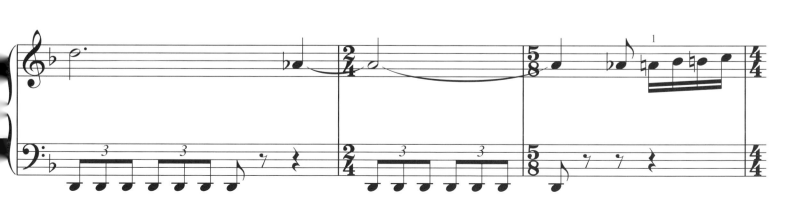

Twice as fast

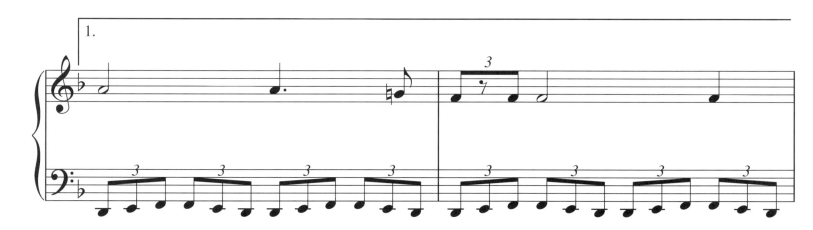

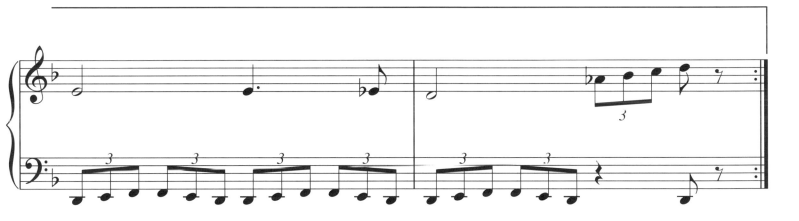

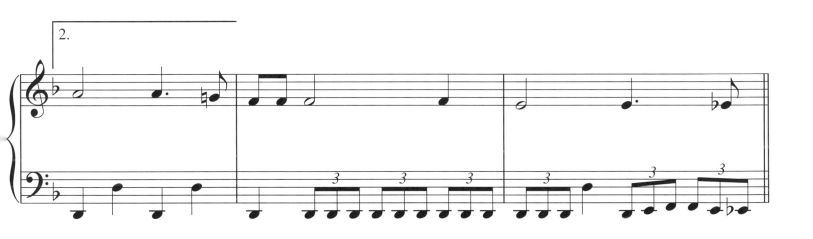

Half as fast

Quickly

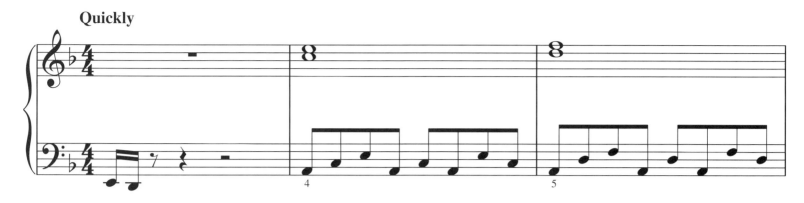

Moderately slow, majestically

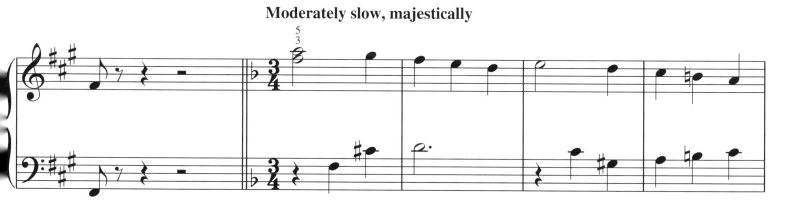

Moderately

ANGRY AND DEAD AGAIN

Music by RODRIGO SANCHEZ,
GABRIELA QUINTERO and HANS ZIMMER

Moderately

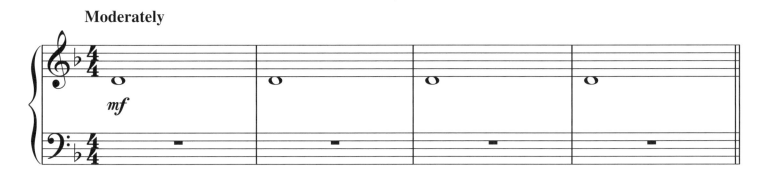

Slightly faster

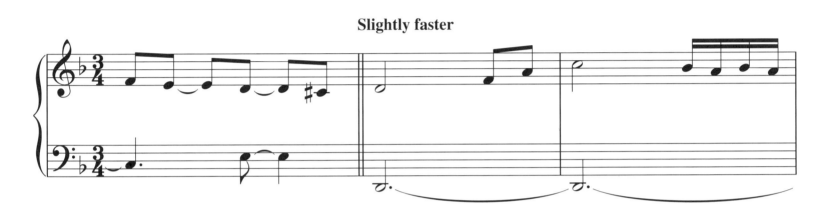

92

Twice as fast

END CREDITS

Music by HANS ZIMMER

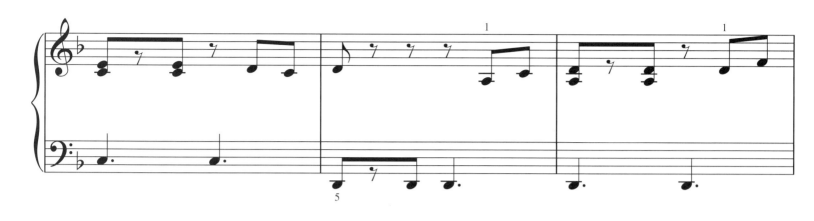

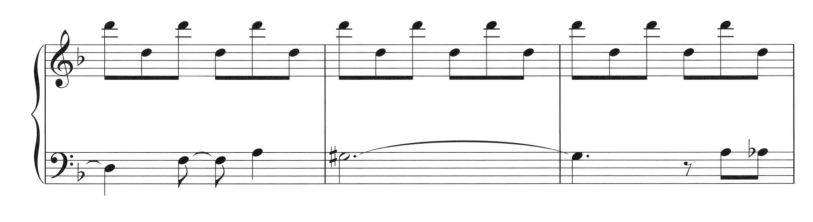